How Are You?

HERRON

Hello

How are you today?

Introduction

How are you really? It's a question that a good friend might ask, but not often one we ask ourselves. There are good days and bad days, fun times and sad times – that's just life – but does it all add up to a 'good life' for you? It can be hard to tell when we are either too caught up in the story of the moment or fail to observe the actual moment, instead letting the tide of life drag us any which way.

This easy-to-use journal can help you regain control, providing a big-picture view of how you are doing over a period of 90 days and a simple tool to track how successfully you have been able to observe the moments of your life. It's only though observation – mindful attention – that we learn to understand what we need, and thus to make everyday choices that support us.

This journal provides a means of seeing – how are you? – and a means of being – living your best life.

How This Journal Works

Fill in a page a day for 90 days, following the carefully designed prompts which help you reflect on your well-being. Ninety days is not a long time, so it's doable (no excuses!). And the reward at the end is worth the effort: a big-picture perspective on your life and how you are doing. Chances are, you are doing pretty well. But if not, this journal will help you understand why and where to focus as you continue to grow and evolve.

Complete your journal in the evening before bed, or if you prefer mornings then do it first thing, reflecting on the day before.

Filling It In

Put your reflections into context by making a note of the day of the week (Mondays can be hard for some of us!) and date, plus a short description of what you did that day. Keep it short and simple, just a list of the day's main activities.

Each day is allocated two spreads. The first is divided into four key areas: My Awareness, Body Connect, My Feelings and My Way. These sections are explained on the following pages. The second spread allows you a little extra space to for 'overflow' (any thoughts or reflections not covered elsewhere), and to set an intention for tomorrow.

When you have finished your entry for the day give it an overall rating out of 10, and chose just two words to summarise your day. If you have a bad day, just remember: one swallow does not a summer make. Review your average scores at the end of the 90-day period.

We've marked up a sample journal entry on pages 20-21, which you can use for reference or inspiration.

My Awareness

My Awareness is a place to flex your mindfulness muscle by recording three simple observations from the day.

Mindful observations can be absolutely anything to which you have deliberately paid attention in the moment. Commonly, they are observations from nature (a flower or an animal sighting), your own thoughts or interactions with others, sensory things (smells or sounds, for example) that trigger memories, or other visual prompts – things that you see in the world around you.

Use this section to practise your skills of observation (what you see), selectivity (what you choose to pay attention to), objectivity (training your brain to see without the mental chitter chatter) and engagement (being aware).

In this section too, there is space for you to record something that you are grateful for from the day. It can be anything, big or tiny, so try to think of something even on a bad day.

And finally, tick the box: have you been most connected to the past, present or future today? Consider that dwelling in the past often leads to a sad mindset where we rue missed opportunities, whereas looking too much to the future gives rise to anxious thoughts and worries about 'what if?' Being most connected to the present is the sweet spot: the present moment is where we live our lives, after all. Aim for more ticks in this box, if you can.

Body Connect

How we feel in our bodies is a large part of how we feel in ourselves day to day. If our bodies feel strong and capable, we tend to feel the same. If our bodies are tired and weak, our minds follow suit.

Use this section to track how you are feeling today. Circle the word or words that resonate, or use the space to add your own body-feeling.

For strong, healthy bodies we all know the basic rules: drink water, eat good food, minimise alcohol, exercise, stretch and meditate. To use this section of the journal, first set yourself some simple goals (see facing page), so that you have something against which to track your progress. It could be: drink eight glasses of water per day, eat five serves of vegetables per day, have three alcohol-free days per week (or drink less than 10 units per week), exercise for 30 minutes per day, stretch for 10 minutes daily, meditate every day (set a time if you wish). Track your progress against your goals (not anyone else's).

Lastly, what was your physical highlight today?

Try to think of something, even if it's just playing with the kids for 15 minutes. Your body needs you, so give it a high five each day.

My Body Connect Goals

MY GOALS ABOUT DRINKING WATER

MY GOALS ABOUT FOOD

MY GOALS ABOUT ALCOHOL

MY GOALS ABOUT EXERCISE

MY GOALS ABOUT STRETCHING

MY GOALS ABOUT MEDITATION

My Feelings

Here's a chance to monitor the big question: how are you feeling today?

Circle the words that resonate with how you felt first thing in the morning, or if none of those feel quite right, add your own words.

Then take a moment to jot down the dominant feeling of the day. Of course, you won't have felt this way every single moment, but at the end of the day can you pinpoint a feeling that best summed up today?

Next consider your most challenging feeling of the day. You might have felt frustrated or angry about something. Make sure you dig deep not only to admit to the feeling, but to reflect on why you felt that way too.

And on the happy side of the coin, what was your best feeling today and why?

Tracking both the challenging and the positive emotions teaches us perspective (it's never all bad) and encourages honest and objective reflection. Reflection builds self-awareness and self-confidence, and it's here that we find happiness rather than in the fleeting 'good times'.

USE THIS PAGE TO REFLECT ON FEELINGS THAT YOU WOULD LIKE TO INVITE MORE (AND LESS) OF INTO YOUR LIFE.

My Way

This section provides an opportunity to set some simple goals for how you want to live and what your priorities are.

To complete this section of the journal, you'll need to get some basic goals in place (see following pages).

Start each day with an intention. Setting a daily intention is a great way to achieve. It doesn't have to be a big thing. It could be to eat a salad or phone your mum, or perhaps be to be kind to someone who irks you. Write some ideas for intentions on page 14. Every day that you use this journal, you can set an intention and review it the next day.

Embrace the best time of the day. Even if you are not exactly a morning person, establish a simple and positive morning ritual that works for you. It might be a glass of lemon water, a stretching routine or walk, or journaling. Make sure that you set yourself a goal that's achievable with regard to whatever else is going on in your life. Start small so you can be successful. Fill out your morning ritual on page 15.

Set yourself a goal around social media. Try to be specific, perhaps setting a time limit per day or giving yourself a day off per week. Whatever works for you. And keep yourself accountable. You can do it. Write down your social media goals on page 15.

Connecting with others should be easy and enjoyable, but somehow it often gets put to the bottom of the priority pile. Everyone is different, but what do healthy and rewarding relationships with others look like for you? Decide on the people that you want to catch up with regularly, and on some parameters for frequency. Write down your goals for connection with others on page 16 and track how you are going in the journal.

Think of a single, biggish goal. Maybe it's something you want to accomplish, like making a grade in a hobby, or pursuing a new interest.

It could be a relationship you want to nurture or a new skill to learn. It could something that you want to buy, or perhaps it's a way in which you'd like to evolve as a person. Write it down on page 17 and try to do one little thing each day towards your goal.

Lastly, consider what you think are the most important elements you need to live a satisfying life. What makes your life satisfying? Write some 'I believe' statements about this on page 17, and when you complete your daily journal consider how you felt you were tracking against these statements.

There's always room for improvement, so if you think there is anything you could have done better make a note of it in this section.

And finally, tomorrow is a whole new day to enjoy and reflect upon – set your intention!

IDEAS FOR MY INTENTIONS

MY MORNING RITUAL

MY SOCIAL MEDIA GOALS

MY GOALS FOR CONNECTING WITH OTHERS

MY SINGLE BIGGISH GOAL

MY IDEA OF LIFE SATISFACTION (I BELIEVE...)

What happened today?

DAY (M) T W T F S S

DATE 24 / 11 / 2021

Yoga, coffee with Jane, work

My Awareness

Mindful observations

1. *Jane has a really calm attitude towards her kids which inspires me.*

2. *I saw a blue-tongue lizard in the front yard. Could it be my spirit animal?*

3. *Smell of citrus trees today reminded me of mum's lemon meringue pie.*

I am grateful for

Friendship with Jane, how good yoga makes me feel, myself for making the effort.

Today, I felt most connected to the

○ PAST ☑ PRESENT ○ FUTURE

Body Connect

How did I feel in my body?

TIRED · WEAK · SLOW · CAPABLE · STRONG · MOBILE · (ENERGISED)

How did I do today?

	1	2	3	4	5
WATER	1	2	3	4	(5)
FOOD	1	2	(3)	4	5
ALCOHOL	1	(2)	3	4	5
EXERCISE	1	2	3	(4)	5
STRETCHING	1	2	3	4	(5)
MEDITATION	1	2	3	4	(5)

Physical highlight

Touched the back of my heels in forward bend!

Two-word check in

hopeful, confident

TODAY WAS A 8/10

My Feelings

My morning mood was

- TIRED
- SLEEPY
- STRESSED
- PESSIMISTIC
- AVERAGE
- EXCITED
- OPTIMISTIC (circled)
- CALM

Dominant feeling today

Connected

Challenging feeling (and why)

Slightly frustrated with myself for having wine tonight when I didn't need to.

Best feeling (and why)

Connecting with a friend made me feel joy and togetherness.

My Way

How did I do today?

SET INTENTION
1 2 3 4 (5)

MORNING RITUAL
1 2 3 4 (5)

SOCIAL MEDIA USE
1 (2) 3 4 5

CONNECTING WITH OTHERS
1 2 3 (4) 5

WORK TOWARDS A BIG GOAL
1 2 3 4 (5)

SENSE OF SATISFACTION
1 2 3 (4) 5

How could I have done better?

Put down the phone and wine bottle in the evening...

90 Days Starts Now!

What happened today?

DAY M T W T F S S

DATE / /

My Awareness

Mindful observations

1.

2.

3.

I am grateful for

Today, I felt most connected to the

◯ PAST ◯ PRESENT ◯ FUTURE

Body Connect

How did I feel in my body?

- TIRED
- WEAK
- SLOW
- CAPABLE
- STRONG
- MOBILE
- ENERGISED

How did I do today?

WATER
1 2 3 4 5

FOOD
1 2 3 4 5

ALCOHOL
1 2 3 4 5

EXERCISE
1 2 3 4 5

STRETCHING
1 2 3 4 5

MEDITATION
1 2 3 4 5

Physical highlight

Two-word check in

TODAY WAS A /10

My Feelings

My morning mood was

- TIRED
- SLEEPY
- STRESSED
- PESSIMISTIC
- AVERAGE
- EXCITED
- OPTIMISTIC
- CALM

Dominant feeling today

Challenging feeling (and why)

Best feeling (and why)

My Way

How did I do today?

SET INTENTION
1 2 3 4 5

MORNING RITUAL
1 2 3 4 5

SOCIAL MEDIA USE
1 2 3 4 5

CONNECTING WITH OTHERS
1 2 3 4 5

WORK TOWARDS A BIG GOAL
1 2 3 4 5

SENSE OF SATISFACTION
1 2 3 4 5

How could I have done better?

Overflow from today

Intention for tomorrow

What happened today?

DAY M T W T F S S

DATE / /

My Awareness

Mindful observations

1.

2.

3.

I am grateful for

Today, I felt most connected to the

◯ PAST ◯ PRESENT ◯ FUTURE

Body Connect

How did I feel in my body?

- TIRED
- WEAK
- SLOW
- CAPABLE
- STRONG
- MOBILE
- ENERGISED

How did I do today?

WATER

1 2 3 4 5

FOOD

1 2 3 4 5

ALCOHOL

1 2 3 4 5

EXERCISE

1 2 3 4 5

STRETCHING

1 2 3 4 5

MEDITATION

1 2 3 4 5

Physical highlight

Two-word check in

TODAY WAS A

/10

My Feelings

My morning mood was

- TIRED
- SLEEPY
- STRESSED
- PESSIMISTIC
- AVERAGE
- EXCITED
- OPTIMISTIC
- CALM

Dominant feeling today

Challenging feeling (and why)

Best feeling (and why)

My Way

How did I do today?

SET INTENTION
1 2 3 4 5

MORNING RITUAL
1 2 3 4 5

SOCIAL MEDIA USE
1 2 3 4 5

CONNECTING WITH OTHERS
1 2 3 4 5

WORK TOWARDS A BIG GOAL
1 2 3 4 5

SENSE OF SATISFACTION
1 2 3 4 5

How could I have done better?

Overflow from today

Intention for tomorrow

What happened today?

DAY M T W T F S S

DATE / /

My Awareness

Mindful observations

1.

2.

3.

I am grateful for

Today, I felt most connected to the

◯ PAST ◯ PRESENT ◯ FUTURE

Body Connect

How did I feel in my body?

- TIRED
- WEAK
- SLOW
- CAPABLE
- STRONG
- MOBILE
- ENERGISED

How did I do today?

WATER
1 2 3 4 5

FOOD
1 2 3 4 5

ALCOHOL
1 2 3 4 5

EXERCISE
1 2 3 4 5

STRETCHING
1 2 3 4 5

MEDITATION
1 2 3 4 5

Physical highlight

Two-word check in

TODAY WAS A

/10

My Feelings

My morning mood was

- TIRED
- SLEEPY
- STRESSED
- PESSIMISTIC
- AVERAGE
- EXCITED
- OPTIMISTIC
- CALM

Dominant feeling today

Challenging feeling (and why)

Best feeling (and why)

My Way

How did I do today?

SET INTENTION
1 2 3 4 5

MORNING RITUAL
1 2 3 4 5

SOCIAL MEDIA USE
1 2 3 4 5

CONNECTING WITH OTHERS
1 2 3 4 5

WORK TOWARDS A BIG GOAL
1 2 3 4 5

SENSE OF SATISFACTION
1 2 3 4 5

How could I have done better?

Overflow from today

Intention for tomorrow

What happened today?

DAY M T W T F S S

DATE / /

My Awareness

Mindful observations

1.

2.

3.

I am grateful for

Today, I felt most connected to the

◯ PAST ◯ ♥ PRESENT ◯ FUTURE

Body Connect

How did I feel in my body?

● TIRED ● WEAK ● SLOW ● CAPABLE ● STRONG ● MOBILE ● ENERGISED

How did I do today?

WATER
1 2 3 4 5

FOOD
1 2 3 4 5

ALCOHOL
1 2 3 4 5

EXERCISE
1 2 3 4 5

STRETCHING
1 2 3 4 5

MEDITATION
1 2 3 4 5

Physical highlight

Two-word check in

TODAY WAS A

/10

My Feelings

My morning mood was

- TIRED
- SLEEPY
- STRESSED
- PESSIMISTIC
- AVERAGE
- EXCITED
- OPTIMISTIC
- CALM

Dominant feeling today

Challenging feeling (and why)

Best feeling (and why)

My Way

How did I do today?

SET INTENTION
1 2 3 4 5

MORNING RITUAL
1 2 3 4 5

SOCIAL MEDIA USE
1 2 3 4 5

CONNECTING WITH OTHERS
1 2 3 4 5

WORK TOWARDS A BIG GOAL
1 2 3 4 5

SENSE OF SATISFACTION
1 2 3 4 5

How could I have done better?

Overflow from today

Intention for tomorrow

What happened today?

DAY M T W T F S S

DATE / /

My Awareness

Mindful observations

1.

2.

3.

I am grateful for

Today, I felt most connected to the

PAST PRESENT FUTURE

Body Connect

How did I feel in my body?

TIRED WEAK SLOW CAPABLE STRONG MOBILE ENERGISED

How did I do today?

WATER
1 2 3 4 5

FOOD
1 2 3 4 5

ALCOHOL
1 2 3 4 5

EXERCISE
1 2 3 4 5

STRETCHING
1 2 3 4 5

MEDITATION
1 2 3 4 5

Physical highlight

Two-word check in

TODAY WAS A

/10

My Feelings

My morning mood was

- TIRED
- SLEEPY
- STRESSED
- PESSIMISTIC
- AVERAGE
- EXCITED
- OPTIMISTIC
- CALM

Dominant feeling today

Challenging feeling (and why)

Best feeling (and why)

My Way

How did I do today?

SET INTENTION
1 2 3 4 5

MORNING RITUAL
1 2 3 4 5

SOCIAL MEDIA USE
1 2 3 4 5

CONNECTING WITH OTHERS
1 2 3 4 5

WORK TOWARDS A BIG GOAL
1 2 3 4 5

SENSE OF SATISFACTION
1 2 3 4 5

How could I have done better?

Overflow from today

Intention for tomorrow

What happened today?

DAY M T W T F S S

DATE / /

My Awareness

Mindful observations

1.

2.

3.

I am grateful for

Today, I felt most connected to the

PAST PRESENT FUTURE

Body Connect

How did I feel in my body?

TIRED WEAK SLOW CAPABLE STRONG MOBILE ENERGISED

How did I do today?

WATER
1 2 3 4 5

FOOD
1 2 3 4 5

ALCOHOL
1 2 3 4 5

EXERCISE
1 2 3 4 5

STRETCHING
1 2 3 4 5

MEDITATION
1 2 3 4 5

Physical highlight

Two-word check in

TODAY WAS A

/10

My Feelings

My morning mood was

- TIRED
- SLEEPY
- STRESSED
- PESSIMISTIC
- AVERAGE
- EXCITED
- OPTIMISTIC
- CALM

Dominant feeling today

Challenging feeling (and why)

Best feeling (and why)

My Way

How did I do today?

SET INTENTION
1 2 3 4 5

MORNING RITUAL
1 2 3 4 5

SOCIAL MEDIA USE
1 2 3 4 5

CONNECTING WITH OTHERS
1 2 3 4 5

WORK TOWARDS A BIG GOAL
1 2 3 4 5

SENSE OF SATISFACTION
1 2 3 4 5

How could I have done better?

Overflow from today

Intention for tomorrow

What happened today?

DAY M T W T F S S

DATE / /

My Awareness

Mindful observations

1.

2.

3.

I am grateful for

Today, I felt most connected to the

◯ PAST ◯ PRESENT ◯ FUTURE

Body Connect

How did I feel in my body?

- TIRED
- WEAK
- SLOW
- CAPABLE
- STRONG
- MOBILE
- ENERGISED

How did I do today?

WATER
1 2 3 4 5

FOOD
1 2 3 4 5

ALCOHOL
1 2 3 4 5

EXERCISE
1 2 3 4 5

STRETCHING
1 2 3 4 5

MEDITATION
1 2 3 4 5

Physical highlight

Two-word check in

TODAY WAS A

/10

My Feelings

My morning mood was

- TIRED
- SLEEPY
- STRESSED
- PESSIMISTIC
- AVERAGE
- EXCITED
- OPTIMISTIC
- CALM

Dominant feeling today

Challenging feeling (and why)

Best feeling (and why)

My Way

How did I do today?

SET INTENTION
1 2 3 4 5

MORNING RITUAL
1 2 3 4 5

SOCIAL MEDIA USE
1 2 3 4 5

CONNECTING WITH OTHERS
1 2 3 4 5

WORK TOWARDS A BIG GOAL
1 2 3 4 5

SENSE OF SATISFACTION
1 2 3 4 5

How could I have done better?

Overflow from today

Intention for tomorrow

What happened today?

DAY M T W T F S S

DATE / /

My Awareness

Mindful observations

1.

2.

3.

I am grateful for

Today, I felt most connected to the

◯ PAST ◯ PRESENT ◯ FUTURE

Body Connect

How did I feel in my body?

TIRED • WEAK • SLOW • CAPABLE • STRONG • MOBILE • ENERGISED

How did I do today?

WATER
1 2 3 4 5

FOOD
1 2 3 4 5

ALCOHOL
1 2 3 4 5

EXERCISE
1 2 3 4 5

STRETCHING
1 2 3 4 5

MEDITATION
1 2 3 4 5

Physical highlight

Two-word check in

TODAY WAS A

/10

My Feelings

My morning mood was

- TIRED
- SLEEPY
- STRESSED
- PESSIMISTIC
- AVERAGE
- EXCITED
- OPTIMISTIC
- CALM

Dominant feeling today

Challenging feeling (and why)

Best feeling (and why)

My Way

How did I do today?

SET INTENTION
1 2 3 4 5

MORNING RITUAL
1 2 3 4 5

SOCIAL MEDIA USE
1 2 3 4 5

CONNECTING WITH OTHERS
1 2 3 4 5

WORK TOWARDS A BIG GOAL
1 2 3 4 5

SENSE OF SATISFACTION
1 2 3 4 5

How could I have done better?

Overflow from today

Intention for tomorrow

What happened today?

DAY M T W T F S S

DATE / /

My Awareness

Mindful observations

1.

2.

3.

I am grateful for

Today, I felt most connected to the

◯ PAST ◯ PRESENT ◯ FUTURE

Body Connect

How did I feel in my body?

- TIRED
- WEAK
- SLOW
- CAPABLE
- STRONG
- MOBILE
- ENERGISED

How did I do today?

WATER
1 2 3 4 5

FOOD
1 2 3 4 5

ALCOHOL
1 2 3 4 5

EXERCISE
1 2 3 4 5

STRETCHING
1 2 3 4 5

MEDITATION
1 2 3 4 5

Physical highlight

Two-word check in

TODAY WAS A

/10

My Feelings

My morning mood was

- TIRED
- SLEEPY
- STRESSED
- PESSIMISTIC
- AVERAGE
- EXCITED
- OPTIMISTIC
- CALM

Dominant feeling today

Challenging feeling (and why)

Best feeling (and why)

My Way

How did I do today?

SET INTENTION
1 2 3 4 5

MORNING RITUAL
1 2 3 4 5

SOCIAL MEDIA USE
1 2 3 4 5

CONNECTING WITH OTHERS
1 2 3 4 5

WORK TOWARDS A BIG GOAL
1 2 3 4 5

SENSE OF SATISFACTION
1 2 3 4 5

How could I have done better?

Overflow from today

Intention for tomorrow

What happened today?

DAY M T W T F S S

DATE / /

My Awareness

Mindful observations

1.

2.

3.

I am grateful for

Today, I felt most connected to the

PAST PRESENT FUTURE

Body Connect

How did I feel in my body?

TIRED
WEAK
SLOW
CAPABLE
STRONG
MOBILE
ENERGISED

How did I do today?

WATER
1 2 3 4 5

FOOD
1 2 3 4 5

ALCOHOL
1 2 3 4 5

EXERCISE
1 2 3 4 5

STRETCHING
1 2 3 4 5

MEDITATION
1 2 3 4 5

Physical highlight

Two-word check in

TODAY WAS A

/10

My Feelings

My morning mood was

- TIRED
- SLEEPY
- STRESSED
- PESSIMISTIC
- AVERAGE
- EXCITED
- OPTIMISTIC
- CALM

Dominant feeling today

Challenging feeling (and why)

Best feeling (and why)

My Way

How did I do today?

SET INTENTION
1 2 3 4 5

MORNING RITUAL
1 2 3 4 5

SOCIAL MEDIA USE
1 2 3 4 5

CONNECTING WITH OTHERS
1 2 3 4 5

WORK TOWARDS A BIG GOAL
1 2 3 4 5

SENSE OF SATISFACTION
1 2 3 4 5

How could I have done better?

Overflow from today

Intention for tomorrow

What happened today?

DAY M T W T F S S

DATE / /

My Awareness

Mindful observations

1.

2.

3.

I am grateful for

Today, I felt most connected to the

PAST PRESENT FUTURE

Body Connect

How did I feel in my body?

TIRED WEAK SLOW CAPABLE STRONG MOBILE ENERGISED

How did I do today?

WATER
1 2 3 4 5

FOOD
1 2 3 4 5

ALCOHOL
1 2 3 4 5

EXERCISE
1 2 3 4 5

STRETCHING
1 2 3 4 5

MEDITATION
1 2 3 4 5

Physical highlight

Two-word check in

TODAY WAS A
/10

My Feelings

My morning mood was

- TIRED
- SLEEPY
- STRESSED
- PESSIMISTIC
- AVERAGE
- EXCITED
- OPTIMISTIC
- CALM

Dominant feeling today

Challenging feeling (and why)

Best feeling (and why)

My Way

How did I do today?

SET INTENTION
1 2 3 4 5

MORNING RITUAL
1 2 3 4 5

SOCIAL MEDIA USE
1 2 3 4 5

CONNECTING WITH OTHERS
1 2 3 4 5

WORK TOWARDS A BIG GOAL
1 2 3 4 5

SENSE OF SATISFACTION
1 2 3 4 5

How could I have done better?

Overflow from today

Intention for tomorrow

What happened today?

DAY M T W T F S S

DATE / /

My Awareness

Mindful observations

1.

2.

3.

I am grateful for

Today, I felt most connected to the

◯ PAST ◯ PRESENT ◯ FUTURE

Body Connect

How did I feel in my body?

- TIRED
- WEAK
- SLOW
- CAPABLE
- STRONG
- MOBILE
- ENERGISED

How did I do today?

WATER
1 2 3 4 5

FOOD
1 2 3 4 5

ALCOHOL
1 2 3 4 5

EXERCISE
1 2 3 4 5

STRETCHING
1 2 3 4 5

MEDITATION
1 2 3 4 5

Physical highlight

Two-word check in

TODAY WAS A

/10

My Feelings

My morning mood was

- TIRED
- SLEEPY
- STRESSED
- PESSIMISTIC
- AVERAGE
- EXCITED
- OPTIMISTIC
- CALM

Dominant feeling today

Challenging feeling (and why)

Best feeling (and why)

My Way

How did I do today?

SET INTENTION
1 2 3 4 5

MORNING RITUAL
1 2 3 4 5

SOCIAL MEDIA USE
1 2 3 4 5

CONNECTING WITH OTHERS
1 2 3 4 5

WORK TOWARDS A BIG GOAL
1 2 3 4 5

SENSE OF SATISFACTION
1 2 3 4 5

How could I have done better?

Overflow from today

Intention for tomorrow

What happened today?

DAY M T W T F S S

DATE / /

My Awareness

Mindful observations

1.

2.

3.

I am grateful for

Today, I felt most connected to the

PAST PRESENT FUTURE

Body Connect

How did I feel in my body?

- TIRED
- WEAK
- SLOW
- CAPABLE
- STRONG
- MOBILE
- ENERGISED

How did I do today?

WATER
1 2 3 4 5

FOOD
1 2 3 4 5

ALCOHOL
1 2 3 4 5

EXERCISE
1 2 3 4 5

STRETCHING
1 2 3 4 5

MEDITATION
1 2 3 4 5

Physical highlight

Two-word check in

TODAY WAS A

/10

My Feelings

My morning mood was

- TIRED
- SLEEPY
- STRESSED
- PESSIMISTIC
- AVERAGE
- EXCITED
- OPTIMISTIC
- CALM

Dominant feeling today

Challenging feeling (and why)

Best feeling (and why)

My Way

How did I do today?

SET INTENTION
1 2 3 4 5

MORNING RITUAL
1 2 3 4 5

SOCIAL MEDIA USE
1 2 3 4 5

CONNECTING WITH OTHERS
1 2 3 4 5

WORK TOWARDS A BIG GOAL
1 2 3 4 5

SENSE OF SATISFACTION
1 2 3 4 5

How could I have done better?

Overflow from today

Intention for tomorrow

What happened today?

DAY M T W T F S S

DATE / /

My Awareness

Mindful observations

1.

2.

3.

I am grateful for

Today, I felt most connected to the

◯ PAST ◯ PRESENT ◯ FUTURE

Body Connect

How did I feel in my body?

TIRED · WEAK · SLOW · CAPABLE · STRONG · MOBILE · ENERGISED

How did I do today?

WATER
1 2 3 4 5

FOOD
1 2 3 4 5

ALCOHOL
1 2 3 4 5

EXERCISE
1 2 3 4 5

STRETCHING
1 2 3 4 5

MEDITATION
1 2 3 4 5

Physical highlight

Two-word check in

TODAY WAS A

/10

My Feelings

My morning mood was

- TIRED
- SLEEPY
- STRESSED
- PESSIMISTIC
- AVERAGE
- EXCITED
- OPTIMISTIC
- CALM

Dominant feeling today

Challenging feeling (and why)

Best feeling (and why)

My Way

How did I do today?

SET INTENTION
1 2 3 4 5

MORNING RITUAL
1 2 3 4 5

SOCIAL MEDIA USE
1 2 3 4 5

CONNECTING WITH OTHERS
1 2 3 4 5

WORK TOWARDS A BIG GOAL
1 2 3 4 5

SENSE OF SATISFACTION
1 2 3 4 5

How could I have done better?

Overflow from today

Intention for tomorrow

What happened today?

DAY M T W T F S S

DATE / /

My Awareness

Mindful observations

1.

2.

3.

I am grateful for

Today, I felt most connected to the

PAST PRESENT FUTURE

Body Connect

How did I feel in my body?

TIRED WEAK SLOW CAPABLE STRONG MOBILE ENERGISED

How did I do today?

WATER
1 2 3 4 5

FOOD
1 2 3 4 5

ALCOHOL
1 2 3 4 5

EXERCISE
1 2 3 4 5

STRETCHING
1 2 3 4 5

MEDITATION
1 2 3 4 5

Physical highlight

Two-word check in

TODAY WAS A
/10

My Feelings

My morning mood was

- TIRED
- SLEEPY
- STRESSED
- PESSIMISTIC
- AVERAGE
- EXCITED
- OPTIMISTIC
- CALM

Dominant feeling today

Challenging feeling (and why)

Best feeling (and why)

My Way

How did I do today?

SET INTENTION
1 2 3 4 5

MORNING RITUAL
1 2 3 4 5

SOCIAL MEDIA USE
1 2 3 4 5

CONNECTING WITH OTHERS
1 2 3 4 5

WORK TOWARDS A BIG GOAL
1 2 3 4 5

SENSE OF SATISFACTION
1 2 3 4 5

How could I have done better?

Overflow from today

Intention for tomorrow

What happened today?

DAY M T W T F S S

DATE / /

My Awareness

Mindful observations

1.

2.

3.

I am grateful for

Today, I felt most connected to the

PAST PRESENT FUTURE

Body Connect

How did I feel in my body?

TIRED WEAK SLOW CAPABLE STRONG MOBILE ENERGISED

How did I do today?

WATER
1 2 3 4 5

FOOD
1 2 3 4 5

ALCOHOL
1 2 3 4 5

EXERCISE
1 2 3 4 5

STRETCHING
1 2 3 4 5

MEDITATION
1 2 3 4 5

Physical highlight

Two-word check in

TODAY WAS A

/10

My Feelings

My morning mood was

- TIRED
- SLEEPY
- STRESSED
- PESSIMISTIC
- AVERAGE
- EXCITED
- OPTIMISTIC
- CALM

Dominant feeling today

Challenging feeling (and why)

Best feeling (and why)

My Way

How did I do today?

SET INTENTION
1 2 3 4 5

MORNING RITUAL
1 2 3 4 5

SOCIAL MEDIA USE
1 2 3 4 5

CONNECTING WITH OTHERS
1 2 3 4 5

WORK TOWARDS A BIG GOAL
1 2 3 4 5

SENSE OF SATISFACTION
1 2 3 4 5

How could I have done better?

Overflow from today

Intention for tomorrow

What happened today?

DAY M T W T F S S

DATE / /

My Awareness

Mindful observations

1.

2.

3.

I am grateful for

Today, I felt most connected to the

◯ PAST ◯ PRESENT ◯ FUTURE

Body Connect

How did I feel in my body?

- TIRED
- WEAK
- SLOW
- CAPABLE
- STRONG
- MOBILE
- ENERGISED

How did I do today?

WATER
1 2 3 4 5

FOOD
1 2 3 4 5

ALCOHOL
1 2 3 4 5

EXERCISE
1 2 3 4 5

STRETCHING
1 2 3 4 5

MEDITATION
1 2 3 4 5

Physical highlight

Two-word check in

TODAY WAS A
/10

My Feelings

My morning mood was

- TIRED
- SLEEPY
- STRESSED
- PESSIMISTIC
- AVERAGE
- EXCITED
- OPTIMISTIC
- CALM

Dominant feeling today

Challenging feeling (and why)

Best feeling (and why)

My Way

How did I do today?

SET INTENTION
1 2 3 4 5

MORNING RITUAL
1 2 3 4 5

SOCIAL MEDIA USE
1 2 3 4 5

CONNECTING WITH OTHERS
1 2 3 4 5

WORK TOWARDS A BIG GOAL
1 2 3 4 5

SENSE OF SATISFACTION
1 2 3 4 5

How could I have done better?

Overflow from today

Intention for tomorrow

What happened today?

DAY M T W T F S S

DATE / /

My Awareness

Mindful observations

1.

2.

3.

I am grateful for

Today, I felt most connected to the

PAST PRESENT FUTURE

Body Connect

How did I feel in my body?

TIRED WEAK SLOW CAPABLE STRONG MOBILE ENERGISED

How did I do today?

WATER
1 2 3 4 5

FOOD
1 2 3 4 5

ALCOHOL
1 2 3 4 5

EXERCISE
1 2 3 4 5

STRETCHING
1 2 3 4 5

MEDITATION
1 2 3 4 5

Physical highlight

Two-word check in

TODAY WAS A

/10

My Feelings

My morning mood was

- TIRED
- SLEEPY
- STRESSED
- PESSIMISTIC
- AVERAGE
- EXCITED
- OPTIMISTIC
- CALM

Dominant feeling today

Challenging feeling (and why)

Best feeling (and why)

My Way

How did I do today?

SET INTENTION
1 2 3 4 5

MORNING RITUAL
1 2 3 4 5

SOCIAL MEDIA USE
1 2 3 4 5

CONNECTING WITH OTHERS
1 2 3 4 5

WORK TOWARDS A BIG GOAL
1 2 3 4 5

SENSE OF SATISFACTION
1 2 3 4 5

How could I have done better?

Overflow from today

Intention for tomorrow

What happened today?

DAY M T W T F S S

DATE / /

My Awareness

Mindful observations

1.

2.

3.

I am grateful for

Today, I felt most connected to the

PAST PRESENT FUTURE

Body Connect

How did I feel in my body?

TIRED WEAK SLOW CAPABLE STRONG MOBILE ENERGISED

How did I do today?

WATER
1 2 3 4 5

FOOD
1 2 3 4 5

ALCOHOL
1 2 3 4 5

EXERCISE
1 2 3 4 5

STRETCHING
1 2 3 4 5

MEDITATION
1 2 3 4 5

Physical highlight

Two-word check in

TODAY WAS A

/10

My Feelings

My morning mood was

- TIRED
- SLEEPY
- STRESSED
- PESSIMISTIC
- AVERAGE
- EXCITED
- OPTIMISTIC
- CALM

Dominant feeling today

Challenging feeling (and why)

Best feeling (and why)

My Way

How did I do today?

SET INTENTION
1 2 3 4 5

MORNING RITUAL
1 2 3 4 5

SOCIAL MEDIA USE
1 2 3 4 5

CONNECTING WITH OTHERS
1 2 3 4 5

WORK TOWARDS A BIG GOAL
1 2 3 4 5

SENSE OF SATISFACTION
1 2 3 4 5

How could I have done better?

Overflow from today

Intention for tomorrow

What happened today?

DAY M T W T F S S

DATE / /

My Awareness

Mindful observations

1.

2.

3.

I am grateful for

Today, I felt most connected to the

PAST PRESENT FUTURE

Body Connect

How did I feel in my body?

TIRED WEAK SLOW CAPABLE STRONG MOBILE ENERGISED

How did I do today?

WATER
1 2 3 4 5

FOOD
1 2 3 4 5

ALCOHOL
1 2 3 4 5

EXERCISE
1 2 3 4 5

STRETCHING
1 2 3 4 5

MEDITATION
1 2 3 4 5

Physical highlight

Two-word check in

TODAY WAS A

/10

My Feelings

My morning mood was

- TIRED
- SLEEPY
- STRESSED
- PESSIMISTIC
- AVERAGE
- EXCITED
- OPTIMISTIC
- CALM

Dominant feeling today

Challenging feeling (and why)

Best feeling (and why)

My Way

How did I do today?

SET INTENTION
1 2 3 4 5

MORNING RITUAL
1 2 3 4 5

SOCIAL MEDIA USE
1 2 3 4 5

CONNECTING WITH OTHERS
1 2 3 4 5

WORK TOWARDS A BIG GOAL
1 2 3 4 5

SENSE OF SATISFACTION
1 2 3 4 5

How could I have done better?

Overflow from today

Intention for tomorrow

What happened today?

DAY M T W T F S S

DATE / /

My Awareness

Mindful observations

1.

2.

3.

I am grateful for

Today, I felt most connected to the

PAST PRESENT FUTURE

Body Connect

How did I feel in my body?

TIRED WEAK SLOW CAPABLE STRONG MOBILE ENERGISED

How did I do today?

WATER
1 2 3 4 5

FOOD
1 2 3 4 5

ALCOHOL
1 2 3 4 5

EXERCISE
1 2 3 4 5

STRETCHING
1 2 3 4 5

MEDITATION
1 2 3 4 5

Physical highlight

Two-word check in

TODAY WAS A
/10

My Feelings

My morning mood was

- TIRED
- SLEEPY
- STRESSED
- PESSIMISTIC
- AVERAGE
- EXCITED
- OPTIMISTIC
- CALM

Dominant feeling today

Challenging feeling (and why)

Best feeling (and why)

My Way

How did I do today?

SET INTENTION
1 2 3 4 5

MORNING RITUAL
1 2 3 4 5

SOCIAL MEDIA USE
1 2 3 4 5

CONNECTING WITH OTHERS
1 2 3 4 5

WORK TOWARDS A BIG GOAL
1 2 3 4 5

SENSE OF SATISFACTION
1 2 3 4 5

How could I have done better?

Overflow from today

Intention for tomorrow

What happened today?

DAY M T W T F S S

DATE / /

My Awareness

Mindful observations

1.

2.

3.

I am grateful for

Today, I felt most connected to the

PAST PRESENT FUTURE

Body Connect

How did I feel in my body?

TIRED WEAK SLOW CAPABLE STRONG MOBILE ENERGISED

How did I do today?

WATER
1 2 3 4 5

FOOD
1 2 3 4 5

ALCOHOL
1 2 3 4 5

EXERCISE
1 2 3 4 5

STRETCHING
1 2 3 4 5

MEDITATION
1 2 3 4 5

Physical highlight

Two-word check in

TODAY WAS A
/10

My Feelings

My morning mood was

- TIRED
- SLEEPY
- STRESSED
- PESSIMISTIC
- AVERAGE
- EXCITED
- OPTIMISTIC
- CALM

Dominant feeling today

Challenging feeling (and why)

Best feeling (and why)

My Way

How did I do today?

SET INTENTION
1 2 3 4 5

MORNING RITUAL
1 2 3 4 5

SOCIAL MEDIA USE
1 2 3 4 5

CONNECTING WITH OTHERS
1 2 3 4 5

WORK TOWARDS A BIG GOAL
1 2 3 4 5

SENSE OF SATISFACTION
1 2 3 4 5

How could I have done better?

Overflow from today

Intention for tomorrow

What happened today?

DAY M T W T F S S

DATE / /

My Awareness

Mindful observations

1.

2.

3.

I am grateful for

Today, I felt most connected to the

PAST PRESENT FUTURE

Body Connect

How did I feel in my body?

TIRED
WEAK
SLOW
CAPABLE
STRONG
MOBILE
ENERGISED

How did I do today?

WATER
1 2 3 4 5

FOOD
1 2 3 4 5

ALCOHOL
1 2 3 4 5

EXERCISE
1 2 3 4 5

STRETCHING
1 2 3 4 5

MEDITATION
1 2 3 4 5

Physical highlight

Two-word check in

TODAY WAS A

/10

My Feelings

My morning mood was

- TIRED
- SLEEPY
- STRESSED
- PESSIMISTIC
- AVERAGE
- EXCITED
- OPTIMISTIC
- CALM

Dominant feeling today

Challenging feeling (and why)

Best feeling (and why)

My Way

How did I do today?

SET INTENTION
1 2 3 4 5

MORNING RITUAL
1 2 3 4 5

SOCIAL MEDIA USE
1 2 3 4 5

CONNECTING WITH OTHERS
1 2 3 4 5

WORK TOWARDS A BIG GOAL
1 2 3 4 5

SENSE OF SATISFACTION
1 2 3 4 5

How could I have done better?

Overflow from today

Intention for tomorrow

What happened today?

DAY M T W T F S S

DATE / /

My Awareness

Mindful observations

1.

2.

3.

I am grateful for

Today, I felt most connected to the

PAST PRESENT FUTURE

Body Connect

How did I feel in my body?

TIRED WEAK SLOW CAPABLE STRONG MOBILE ENERGISED

How did I do today?

WATER
1 2 3 4 5

FOOD
1 2 3 4 5

ALCOHOL
1 2 3 4 5

EXERCISE
1 2 3 4 5

STRETCHING
1 2 3 4 5

MEDITATION
1 2 3 4 5

Physical highlight

Two-word check in

TODAY WAS A
/10

My Feelings

My morning mood was

- TIRED
- SLEEPY
- STRESSED
- PESSIMISTIC
- AVERAGE
- EXCITED
- OPTIMISTIC
- CALM

Dominant feeling today

Challenging feeling (and why)

Best feeling (and why)

My Way

How did I do today?

SET INTENTION
1 2 3 4 5

MORNING RITUAL
1 2 3 4 5

SOCIAL MEDIA USE
1 2 3 4 5

CONNECTING WITH OTHERS
1 2 3 4 5

WORK TOWARDS A BIG GOAL
1 2 3 4 5

SENSE OF SATISFACTION
1 2 3 4 5

How could I have done better?

Overflow from today

Intention for tomorrow

What happened today?

DAY M T W T F S S

DATE / /

My Awareness

Mindful observations

1.

2.

3.

I am grateful for

Today, I felt most connected to the

PAST PRESENT FUTURE

Body Connect

How did I feel in my body?

TIRED WEAK SLOW CAPABLE STRONG MOBILE ENERGISED

How did I do today?

WATER
1 2 3 4 5

FOOD
1 2 3 4 5

ALCOHOL
1 2 3 4 5

EXERCISE
1 2 3 4 5

STRETCHING
1 2 3 4 5

MEDITATION
1 2 3 4 5

Physical highlight

Two-word check in

TODAY WAS A

/10

My Feelings

My morning mood was

- TIRED
- SLEEPY
- STRESSED
- PESSIMISTIC
- AVERAGE
- EXCITED
- OPTIMISTIC
- CALM

Dominant feeling today

Challenging feeling (and why)

Best feeling (and why)

My Way

How did I do today?

SET INTENTION
1 2 3 4 5

MORNING RITUAL
1 2 3 4 5

SOCIAL MEDIA USE
1 2 3 4 5

CONNECTING WITH OTHERS
1 2 3 4 5

WORK TOWARDS A BIG GOAL
1 2 3 4 5

SENSE OF SATISFACTION
1 2 3 4 5

How could I have done better?

Overflow from today

Intention for tomorrow

What happened today?

DAY M T W T F S S

DATE / /

My Awareness

Mindful observations

1.

2.

3.

I am grateful for

Today, I felt most connected to the

◯ PAST ◯ PRESENT ◯ FUTURE

Body Connect

How did I feel in my body?

TIRED · WEAK · SLOW · CAPABLE · STRONG · MOBILE · ENERGISED

How did I do today?

WATER
1 2 3 4 5

FOOD
1 2 3 4 5

ALCOHOL
1 2 3 4 5

EXERCISE
1 2 3 4 5

STRETCHING
1 2 3 4 5

MEDITATION
1 2 3 4 5

Physical highlight

Two-word check in

TODAY WAS A

/10

My Feelings

My morning mood was

- TIRED
- SLEEPY
- STRESSED
- PESSIMISTIC
- AVERAGE
- EXCITED
- OPTIMISTIC
- CALM

Dominant feeling today

Challenging feeling (and why)

Best feeling (and why)

My Way

How did I do today?

SET INTENTION
1 2 3 4 5

MORNING RITUAL
1 2 3 4 5

SOCIAL MEDIA USE
1 2 3 4 5

CONNECTING WITH OTHERS
1 2 3 4 5

WORK TOWARDS A BIG GOAL
1 2 3 4 5

SENSE OF SATISFACTION
1 2 3 4 5

How could I have done better?

Overflow from today

Intention for tomorrow

What happened today?

DAY M T W T F S S

DATE / /

My Awareness

Mindful observations

1.

2.

3.

I am grateful for

Today, I felt most connected to the

PAST PRESENT FUTURE

Body Connect

How did I feel in my body?

TIRED WEAK SLOW CAPABLE STRONG MOBILE ENERGISED

How did I do today?

WATER
1 2 3 4 5

FOOD
1 2 3 4 5

ALCOHOL
1 2 3 4 5

EXERCISE
1 2 3 4 5

STRETCHING
1 2 3 4 5

MEDITATION
1 2 3 4 5

Physical highlight

Two-word check in

TODAY WAS A /10

My Feelings

My morning mood was

- TIRED
- SLEEPY
- STRESSED
- PESSIMISTIC
- AVERAGE
- EXCITED
- OPTIMISTIC
- CALM

Dominant feeling today

Challenging feeling (and why)

Best feeling (and why)

My Way

How did I do today?

SET INTENTION
1 2 3 4 5

MORNING RITUAL
1 2 3 4 5

SOCIAL MEDIA USE
1 2 3 4 5

CONNECTING WITH OTHERS
1 2 3 4 5

WORK TOWARDS A BIG GOAL
1 2 3 4 5

SENSE OF SATISFACTION
1 2 3 4 5

How could I have done better?

Overflow from today

Intention for tomorrow

What happened today?

DAY M T W T F S S

DATE / /

My Awareness

Mindful observations

1.

2.

3.

I am grateful for

Today, I felt most connected to the

◯ PAST ◯ PRESENT ◯ FUTURE

Body Connect

How did I feel in my body?

- TIRED
- WEAK
- SLOW
- CAPABLE
- STRONG
- MOBILE
- ENERGISED

How did I do today?

WATER
1 2 3 4 5

FOOD
1 2 3 4 5

ALCOHOL
1 2 3 4 5

EXERCISE
1 2 3 4 5

STRETCHING
1 2 3 4 5

MEDITATION
1 2 3 4 5

Physical highlight

Two-word check in

TODAY WAS A

/10

My Feelings

My morning mood was

- TIRED
- SLEEPY
- STRESSED
- PESSIMISTIC
- AVERAGE
- EXCITED
- OPTIMISTIC
- CALM

Dominant feeling today

Challenging feeling (and why)

Best feeling (and why)

My Way

How did I do today?

SET INTENTION
1 2 3 4 5

MORNING RITUAL
1 2 3 4 5

SOCIAL MEDIA USE
1 2 3 4 5

CONNECTING WITH OTHERS
1 2 3 4 5

WORK TOWARDS A BIG GOAL
1 2 3 4 5

SENSE OF SATISFACTION
1 2 3 4 5

How could I have done better?

Overflow from today

Intention for tomorrow

What happened today?

DAY M T W T F S S

DATE / /

My Awareness

Mindful observations

1.

2.

3.

I am grateful for

Today, I felt most connected to the

PAST PRESENT FUTURE

Body Connect

How did I feel in my body?

TIRED WEAK SLOW CAPABLE STRONG MOBILE ENERGISED

How did I do today?

WATER
1 2 3 4 5

FOOD
1 2 3 4 5

ALCOHOL
1 2 3 4 5

EXERCISE
1 2 3 4 5

STRETCHING
1 2 3 4 5

MEDITATION
1 2 3 4 5

Physical highlight

Two-word check in

TODAY WAS A

/10

My Feelings

My morning mood was

- TIRED
- SLEEPY
- STRESSED
- PESSIMISTIC
- AVERAGE
- EXCITED
- OPTIMISTIC
- CALM

Dominant feeling today

Challenging feeling (and why)

Best feeling (and why)

My Way

How did I do today?

SET INTENTION
1 2 3 4 5

MORNING RITUAL
1 2 3 4 5

SOCIAL MEDIA USE
1 2 3 4 5

CONNECTING WITH OTHERS
1 2 3 4 5

WORK TOWARDS A BIG GOAL
1 2 3 4 5

SENSE OF SATISFACTION
1 2 3 4 5

How could I have done better?

Overflow from today

Intention for tomorrow

What happened today?

DAY M T W T F S S

DATE / /

My Awareness

Mindful observations

1.

2.

3.

I am grateful for

Today, I felt most connected to the

◯ PAST ◯ PRESENT ◯ FUTURE

Body Connect

How did I feel in my body?

- TIRED
- WEAK
- SLOW
- CAPABLE
- STRONG
- MOBILE
- ENERGISED

How did I do today?

WATER
1 2 3 4 5

FOOD
1 2 3 4 5

ALCOHOL
1 2 3 4 5

EXERCISE
1 2 3 4 5

STRETCHING
1 2 3 4 5

MEDITATION
1 2 3 4 5

Physical highlight

Two-word check in

TODAY WAS A

/10

My Feelings

My morning mood was

- TIRED
- SLEEPY
- STRESSED
- PESSIMISTIC
- AVERAGE
- EXCITED
- OPTIMISTIC
- CALM

Dominant feeling today

Challenging feeling (and why)

Best feeling (and why)

My Way

How did I do today?

SET INTENTION
1 2 3 4 5

MORNING RITUAL
1 2 3 4 5

SOCIAL MEDIA USE
1 2 3 4 5

CONNECTING WITH OTHERS
1 2 3 4 5

WORK TOWARDS A BIG GOAL
1 2 3 4 5

SENSE OF SATISFACTION
1 2 3 4 5

How could I have done better?

Overflow from today

Intention for tomorrow

What happened today?

DAY M T W T F S S

DATE / /

My Awareness

Mindful observations

1.

2.

3.

I am grateful for

Today, I felt most connected to the

◯ PAST ◯ PRESENT ◯ FUTURE

Body Connect

How did I feel in my body?

TIRED WEAK SLOW CAPABLE STRONG MOBILE ENERGISED

How did I do today?

WATER
1 2 3 4 5

FOOD
1 2 3 4 5

ALCOHOL
1 2 3 4 5

EXERCISE
1 2 3 4 5

STRETCHING
1 2 3 4 5

MEDITATION
1 2 3 4 5

Physical highlight

Two-word check in

TODAY WAS A

/10

My Feelings

My morning mood was

- TIRED
- SLEEPY
- STRESSED
- PESSIMISTIC
- AVERAGE
- EXCITED
- OPTIMISTIC
- CALM

Dominant feeling today

Challenging feeling (and why)

Best feeling (and why)

My Way

How did I do today?

SET INTENTION
1 2 3 4 5

MORNING RITUAL
1 2 3 4 5

SOCIAL MEDIA USE
1 2 3 4 5

CONNECTING WITH OTHERS
1 2 3 4 5

WORK TOWARDS A BIG GOAL
1 2 3 4 5

SENSE OF SATISFACTION
1 2 3 4 5

How could I have done better?

Overflow from today

Intention for tomorrow

What happened today?

DAY M T W T F S S

DATE / /

My Awareness

Mindful observations

1.

2.

3.

I am grateful for

Today, I felt most connected to the

PAST PRESENT FUTURE

Body Connect

How did I feel in my body?

TIRED WEAK SLOW CAPABLE STRONG MOBILE ENERGISED

How did I do today?

WATER
1 2 3 4 5

FOOD
1 2 3 4 5

ALCOHOL
1 2 3 4 5

EXERCISE
1 2 3 4 5

STRETCHING
1 2 3 4 5

MEDITATION
1 2 3 4 5

Physical highlight

Two-word check in

TODAY WAS A
/10

My Feelings

My morning mood was

- TIRED
- SLEEPY
- STRESSED
- PESSIMISTIC
- AVERAGE
- EXCITED
- OPTIMISTIC
- CALM

Dominant feeling today

Challenging feeling (and why)

Best feeling (and why)

My Way

How did I do today?

SET INTENTION
1 2 3 4 5

MORNING RITUAL
1 2 3 4 5

SOCIAL MEDIA USE
1 2 3 4 5

CONNECTING WITH OTHERS
1 2 3 4 5

WORK TOWARDS A BIG GOAL
1 2 3 4 5

SENSE OF SATISFACTION
1 2 3 4 5

How could I have done better?

Overflow from today

Intention for tomorrow

What happened today?

DAY M T W T F S S

DATE / /

My Awareness

Mindful observations

1.

2.

3.

I am grateful for

Today, I felt most connected to the

PAST PRESENT FUTURE

Body Connect

How did I feel in my body?

TIRED WEAK SLOW CAPABLE STRONG MOBILE ENERGISED

How did I do today?

WATER
1 2 3 4 5

FOOD
1 2 3 4 5

ALCOHOL
1 2 3 4 5

EXERCISE
1 2 3 4 5

STRETCHING
1 2 3 4 5

MEDITATION
1 2 3 4 5

Physical highlight

Two-word check in

TODAY WAS A

/10

My Feelings

My morning mood was

- TIRED
- SLEEPY
- STRESSED
- PESSIMISTIC
- AVERAGE
- EXCITED
- OPTIMISTIC
- CALM

Dominant feeling today

Challenging feeling (and why)

Best feeling (and why)

My Way

How did I do today?

SET INTENTION
1 2 3 4 5

MORNING RITUAL
1 2 3 4 5

SOCIAL MEDIA USE
1 2 3 4 5

CONNECTING WITH OTHERS
1 2 3 4 5

WORK TOWARDS A BIG GOAL
1 2 3 4 5

SENSE OF SATISFACTION
1 2 3 4 5

How could I have done better?

Overflow from today

Intention for tomorrow

What happened today?

DAY M T W T F S S

DATE / /

My Awareness

Mindful observations

1.

2.

3.

I am grateful for

Today, I felt most connected to the

PAST PRESENT FUTURE

Body Connect

How did I feel in my body?

TIRED
WEAK
SLOW
CAPABLE
STRONG
MOBILE
ENERGISED

How did I do today?

WATER
1 2 3 4 5

FOOD
1 2 3 4 5

ALCOHOL
1 2 3 4 5

EXERCISE
1 2 3 4 5

STRETCHING
1 2 3 4 5

MEDITATION
1 2 3 4 5

Physical highlight

Two-word check in

TODAY WAS A

/10

My Feelings

My morning mood was

- TIRED
- SLEEPY
- STRESSED
- PESSIMISTIC
- AVERAGE
- EXCITED
- OPTIMISTIC
- CALM

Dominant feeling today

Challenging feeling (and why)

Best feeling (and why)

My Way

How did I do today?

SET INTENTION
1 2 3 4 5

MORNING RITUAL
1 2 3 4 5

SOCIAL MEDIA USE
1 2 3 4 5

CONNECTING WITH OTHERS
1 2 3 4 5

WORK TOWARDS A BIG GOAL
1 2 3 4 5

SENSE OF SATISFACTION
1 2 3 4 5

How could I have done better?

Overflow from today

Intention for tomorrow

What happened today?

DAY M T W T F S S

DATE / /

My Awareness

Mindful observations

1.

2.

3.

I am grateful for

Today, I felt most connected to the

PAST PRESENT FUTURE

Body Connect

How did I feel in my body?

TIRED WEAK SLOW CAPABLE STRONG MOBILE ENERGISED

How did I do today?

WATER
1 2 3 4 5

FOOD
1 2 3 4 5

ALCOHOL
1 2 3 4 5

EXERCISE
1 2 3 4 5

STRETCHING
1 2 3 4 5

MEDITATION
1 2 3 4 5

Physical highlight

Two-word check in

TODAY WAS A
/10

My Feelings

My morning mood was

- TIRED
- SLEEPY
- STRESSED
- PESSIMISTIC
- AVERAGE
- EXCITED
- OPTIMISTIC
- CALM

Dominant feeling today

Challenging feeling (and why)

Best feeling (and why)

My Way

How did I do today?

SET INTENTION
1 2 3 4 5

MORNING RITUAL
1 2 3 4 5

SOCIAL MEDIA USE
1 2 3 4 5

CONNECTING WITH OTHERS
1 2 3 4 5

WORK TOWARDS A BIG GOAL
1 2 3 4 5

SENSE OF SATISFACTION
1 2 3 4 5

How could I have done better?

Overflow from today

Intention for tomorrow

What happened today?

DAY M T W T F S S

DATE / /

My Awareness

Mindful observations

1.

2.

3.

I am grateful for

Today, I felt most connected to the

◯ PAST ◯ PRESENT ◯ FUTURE

Body Connect

How did I feel in my body?

- TIRED
- WEAK
- SLOW
- CAPABLE
- STRONG
- MOBILE
- ENERGISED

How did I do today?

WATER
1 2 3 4 5

FOOD
1 2 3 4 5

ALCOHOL
1 2 3 4 5

EXERCISE
1 2 3 4 5

STRETCHING
1 2 3 4 5

MEDITATION
1 2 3 4 5

Physical highlight

Two-word check in

TODAY WAS A
/10

My Feelings

My morning mood was

- TIRED
- SLEEPY
- STRESSED
- PESSIMISTIC
- AVERAGE
- EXCITED
- OPTIMISTIC
- CALM

Dominant feeling today

Challenging feeling (and why)

Best feeling (and why)

My Way

How did I do today?

SET INTENTION
1 2 3 4 5

MORNING RITUAL
1 2 3 4 5

SOCIAL MEDIA USE
1 2 3 4 5

CONNECTING WITH OTHERS
1 2 3 4 5

WORK TOWARDS A BIG GOAL
1 2 3 4 5

SENSE OF SATISFACTION
1 2 3 4 5

How could I have done better?

Overflow from today

Intention for tomorrow

What happened today?

DAY M T W T F S S

DATE / /

My Awareness

Mindful observations

1.

2.

3.

I am grateful for

Today, I felt most connected to the

PAST PRESENT FUTURE

Body Connect

How did I feel in my body?

TIRED WEAK SLOW CAPABLE STRONG MOBILE ENERGISED

How did I do today?

WATER
1 2 3 4 5

FOOD
1 2 3 4 5

ALCOHOL
1 2 3 4 5

EXERCISE
1 2 3 4 5

STRETCHING
1 2 3 4 5

MEDITATION
1 2 3 4 5

Physical highlight

Two-word check in

TODAY WAS A
/10

My Feelings

My morning mood was

- TIRED
- SLEEPY
- STRESSED
- PESSIMISTIC
- AVERAGE
- EXCITED
- OPTIMISTIC
- CALM

Dominant feeling today

Challenging feeling (and why)

Best feeling (and why)

My Way

How did I do today?

SET INTENTION
1 2 3 4 5

MORNING RITUAL
1 2 3 4 5

SOCIAL MEDIA USE
1 2 3 4 5

CONNECTING WITH OTHERS
1 2 3 4 5

WORK TOWARDS A BIG GOAL
1 2 3 4 5

SENSE OF SATISFACTION
1 2 3 4 5

How could I have done better?

Overflow from today

Intention for tomorrow

What happened today?

DAY M T W T F S S

DATE / /

My Awareness

Mindful observations

1.

2.

3.

I am grateful for

Today, I felt most connected to the

◯ PAST ◯ PRESENT ◯ FUTURE

Body Connect

How did I feel in my body?

TIRED · WEAK · SLOW · CAPABLE · STRONG · MOBILE · ENERGISED

How did I do today?

WATER
1 2 3 4 5

FOOD
1 2 3 4 5

ALCOHOL
1 2 3 4 5

EXERCISE
1 2 3 4 5

STRETCHING
1 2 3 4 5

MEDITATION
1 2 3 4 5

Physical highlight

Two-word check in

TODAY WAS A

/10

My Feelings

My morning mood was

- TIRED
- SLEEPY
- STRESSED
- PESSIMISTIC
- AVERAGE
- EXCITED
- OPTIMISTIC
- CALM

Dominant feeling today

Challenging feeling (and why)

Best feeling (and why)

My Way

How did I do today?

SET INTENTION
1 2 3 4 5

MORNING RITUAL
1 2 3 4 5

SOCIAL MEDIA USE
1 2 3 4 5

CONNECTING WITH OTHERS
1 2 3 4 5

WORK TOWARDS A BIG GOAL
1 2 3 4 5

SENSE OF SATISFACTION
1 2 3 4 5

How could I have done better?

Overflow from today

Intention for tomorrow

What happened today?

DAY M T W T F S S

DATE / /

My Awareness

Mindful observations

1.

2.

3.

I am grateful for

Today, I felt most connected to the

◯ PAST ◯ PRESENT ◯ FUTURE

Body Connect

How did I feel in my body?

- TIRED
- WEAK
- SLOW
- CAPABLE
- STRONG
- MOBILE
- ENERGISED

How did I do today?

WATER
1 2 3 4 5

FOOD
1 2 3 4 5

ALCOHOL
1 2 3 4 5

EXERCISE
1 2 3 4 5

STRETCHING
1 2 3 4 5

MEDITATION
1 2 3 4 5

Physical highlight

Two-word check in

TODAY WAS A

/10

My Feelings

My morning mood was

- TIRED
- SLEEPY
- STRESSED
- PESSIMISTIC
- AVERAGE
- EXCITED
- OPTIMISTIC
- CALM

Dominant feeling today

Challenging feeling (and why)

Best feeling (and why)

My Way

How did I do today?

SET INTENTION
1 2 3 4 5

MORNING RITUAL
1 2 3 4 5

SOCIAL MEDIA USE
1 2 3 4 5

CONNECTING WITH OTHERS
1 2 3 4 5

WORK TOWARDS A BIG GOAL
1 2 3 4 5

SENSE OF SATISFACTION
1 2 3 4 5

How could I have done better?

Overflow from today

Intention for tomorrow

What happened today?

DAY M T W T F S S

DATE / /

My Awareness

Mindful observations

1.

2.

3.

I am grateful for

Today, I felt most connected to the

PAST PRESENT FUTURE

Body Connect

How did I feel in my body?

TIRED WEAK SLOW CAPABLE STRONG MOBILE ENERGISED

How did I do today?

WATER
1 2 3 4 5

FOOD
1 2 3 4 5

ALCOHOL
1 2 3 4 5

EXERCISE
1 2 3 4 5

STRETCHING
1 2 3 4 5

MEDITATION
1 2 3 4 5

Physical highlight

Two-word check in

TODAY WAS A

/10

My Feelings

My morning mood was

- TIRED
- SLEEPY
- STRESSED
- PESSIMISTIC
- AVERAGE
- EXCITED
- OPTIMISTIC
- CALM

Dominant feeling today

Challenging feeling (and why)

Best feeling (and why)

My Way

How did I do today?

SET INTENTION
1 2 3 4 5

MORNING RITUAL
1 2 3 4 5

SOCIAL MEDIA USE
1 2 3 4 5

CONNECTING WITH OTHERS
1 2 3 4 5

WORK TOWARDS A BIG GOAL
1 2 3 4 5

SENSE OF SATISFACTION
1 2 3 4 5

How could I have done better?

Overflow from today

Intention for tomorrow

What happened today?

DAY M T W T F S S

DATE / /

My Awareness

Mindful observations

1.

2.

3.

I am grateful for

Today, I felt most connected to the

PAST PRESENT FUTURE

Body Connect

How did I feel in my body?

TIRED WEAK SLOW CAPABLE STRONG MOBILE ENERGISED

How did I do today?

WATER
1 2 3 4 5

FOOD
1 2 3 4 5

ALCOHOL
1 2 3 4 5

EXERCISE
1 2 3 4 5

STRETCHING
1 2 3 4 5

MEDITATION
1 2 3 4 5

Physical highlight

Two-word check in

TODAY WAS A

/10

My Feelings

My morning mood was

- TIRED
- SLEEPY
- STRESSED
- PESSIMISTIC
- AVERAGE
- EXCITED
- OPTIMISTIC
- CALM

Dominant feeling today

Challenging feeling (and why)

Best feeling (and why)

My Way

How did I do today?

SET INTENTION
1 2 3 4 5

MORNING RITUAL
1 2 3 4 5

SOCIAL MEDIA USE
1 2 3 4 5

CONNECTING WITH OTHERS
1 2 3 4 5

WORK TOWARDS A BIG GOAL
1 2 3 4 5

SENSE OF SATISFACTION
1 2 3 4 5

How could I have done better?

Overflow from today

Intention for tomorrow

What happened today?

DAY M T W T F S S

DATE / /

My Awareness

Mindful observations

1.

2.

3.

I am grateful for

Today, I felt most connected to the

PAST PRESENT FUTURE

Body Connect

How did I feel in my body?

TIRED WEAK SLOW CAPABLE STRONG MOBILE ENERGISED

How did I do today?

WATER
1 2 3 4 5

FOOD
1 2 3 4 5

ALCOHOL
1 2 3 4 5

EXERCISE
1 2 3 4 5

STRETCHING
1 2 3 4 5

MEDITATION
1 2 3 4 5

Physical highlight

Two-word check in

TODAY WAS A

/10

My Feelings

My morning mood was

- TIRED
- SLEEPY
- STRESSED
- PESSIMISTIC
- AVERAGE
- EXCITED
- OPTIMISTIC
- CALM

Dominant feeling today

Challenging feeling (and why)

Best feeling (and why)

My Way

How did I do today?

SET INTENTION
1 2 3 4 5

MORNING RITUAL
1 2 3 4 5

SOCIAL MEDIA USE
1 2 3 4 5

CONNECTING WITH OTHERS
1 2 3 4 5

WORK TOWARDS A BIG GOAL
1 2 3 4 5

SENSE OF SATISFACTION
1 2 3 4 5

How could I have done better?

Overflow from today

Intention for tomorrow

What happened today?

DAY M T W T F S S

DATE / /

My Awareness

Mindful observations

1.

2.

3.

I am grateful for

Today, I felt most connected to the

◯ PAST ◯ PRESENT ◯ FUTURE

Body Connect

How did I feel in my body?

TIRED
WEAK
SLOW
CAPABLE
STRONG
MOBILE
ENERGISED

How did I do today?

WATER
1 2 3 4 5

FOOD
1 2 3 4 5

ALCOHOL
1 2 3 4 5

EXERCISE
1 2 3 4 5

STRETCHING
1 2 3 4 5

MEDITATION
1 2 3 4 5

Physical highlight

Two-word check in

TODAY WAS A

/10

My Feelings

My morning mood was

- TIRED
- SLEEPY
- STRESSED
- PESSIMISTIC
- AVERAGE
- EXCITED
- OPTIMISTIC
- CALM

Dominant feeling today

Challenging feeling (and why)

Best feeling (and why)

My Way

How did I do today?

SET INTENTION
1 2 3 4 5

MORNING RITUAL
1 2 3 4 5

SOCIAL MEDIA USE
1 2 3 4 5

CONNECTING WITH OTHERS
1 2 3 4 5

WORK TOWARDS A BIG GOAL
1 2 3 4 5

SENSE OF SATISFACTION
1 2 3 4 5

How could I have done better?

Overflow from today

Intention for tomorrow

What happened today?

DAY M T W T F S S

DATE / /

My Awareness

Mindful observations

1.

2.

3.

I am grateful for

Today, I felt most connected to the

PAST PRESENT FUTURE

Body Connect

How did I feel in my body?

TIRED WEAK SLOW CAPABLE STRONG MOBILE ENERGISED

How did I do today?

WATER
1 2 3 4 5

FOOD
1 2 3 4 5

ALCOHOL
1 2 3 4 5

EXERCISE
1 2 3 4 5

STRETCHING
1 2 3 4 5

MEDITATION
1 2 3 4 5

Physical highlight

Two-word check in

TODAY WAS A
/10

My Feelings

My morning mood was

- TIRED
- SLEEPY
- STRESSED
- PESSIMISTIC
- AVERAGE
- EXCITED
- OPTIMISTIC
- CALM

Dominant feeling today

Challenging feeling (and why)

Best feeling (and why)

My Way

How did I do today?

SET INTENTION
1 2 3 4 5

MORNING RITUAL
1 2 3 4 5

SOCIAL MEDIA USE
1 2 3 4 5

CONNECTING WITH OTHERS
1 2 3 4 5

WORK TOWARDS A BIG GOAL
1 2 3 4 5

SENSE OF SATISFACTION
1 2 3 4 5

How could I have done better?

Overflow from today

Intention for tomorrow

What happened today?

DAY M T W T F S S

DATE / /

My Awareness

Mindful observations

1.

2.

3.

I am grateful for

Today, I felt most connected to the

PAST PRESENT FUTURE

Body Connect

How did I feel in my body?

TIRED
WEAK
SLOW
CAPABLE
STRONG
MOBILE
ENERGISED

How did I do today?

WATER
1 2 3 4 5

FOOD
1 2 3 4 5

ALCOHOL
1 2 3 4 5

EXERCISE
1 2 3 4 5

STRETCHING
1 2 3 4 5

MEDITATION
1 2 3 4 5

Physical highlight

Two-word check in

TODAY WAS A

/10

My Feelings

My morning mood was

- TIRED
- SLEEPY
- STRESSED
- PESSIMISTIC
- AVERAGE
- EXCITED
- OPTIMISTIC
- CALM

Dominant feeling today

Challenging feeling (and why)

Best feeling (and why)

My Way

How did I do today?

SET INTENTION
1 2 3 4 5

MORNING RITUAL
1 2 3 4 5

SOCIAL MEDIA USE
1 2 3 4 5

CONNECTING WITH OTHERS
1 2 3 4 5

WORK TOWARDS A BIG GOAL
1 2 3 4 5

SENSE OF SATISFACTION
1 2 3 4 5

How could I have done better?

Overflow from today

Intention for tomorrow

What happened today?

DAY M T W T F S S

DATE / /

My Awareness

Mindful observations

1.

2.

3.

I am grateful for

Today, I felt most connected to the

PAST PRESENT FUTURE

Body Connect

How did I feel in my body?

TIRED WEAK SLOW CAPABLE STRONG MOBILE ENERGISED

How did I do today?

WATER
1 2 3 4 5

FOOD
1 2 3 4 5

ALCOHOL
1 2 3 4 5

EXERCISE
1 2 3 4 5

STRETCHING
1 2 3 4 5

MEDITATION
1 2 3 4 5

Physical highlight

Two-word check in

TODAY WAS A

/10

My Feelings

My morning mood was

- TIRED
- SLEEPY
- STRESSED
- PESSIMISTIC
- AVERAGE
- EXCITED
- OPTIMISTIC
- CALM

Dominant feeling today

Challenging feeling (and why)

Best feeling (and why)

My Way

How did I do today?

SET INTENTION
1 2 3 4 5

MORNING RITUAL
1 2 3 4 5

SOCIAL MEDIA USE
1 2 3 4 5

CONNECTING WITH OTHERS
1 2 3 4 5

WORK TOWARDS A BIG GOAL
1 2 3 4 5

SENSE OF SATISFACTION
1 2 3 4 5

How could I have done better?

Overflow from today

Intention for tomorrow

What happened today?

DAY M T W T F S S

DATE / /

My Awareness

Mindful observations

1.

2.

3.

I am grateful for

Today, I felt most connected to the

◯ PAST ◯ PRESENT ◯ FUTURE

Body Connect

How did I feel in my body?

- TIRED
- WEAK
- SLOW
- CAPABLE
- STRONG
- MOBILE
- ENERGISED

How did I do today?

WATER
1 2 3 4 5

FOOD
1 2 3 4 5

ALCOHOL
1 2 3 4 5

EXERCISE
1 2 3 4 5

STRETCHING
1 2 3 4 5

MEDITATION
1 2 3 4 5

Physical highlight

Two-word check in

TODAY WAS A

/10

My Feelings

My morning mood was

- TIRED
- SLEEPY
- STRESSED
- PESSIMISTIC
- AVERAGE
- EXCITED
- OPTIMISTIC
- CALM

Dominant feeling today

Challenging feeling (and why)

Best feeling (and why)

My Way

How did I do today?

SET INTENTION
1 2 3 4 5

MORNING RITUAL
1 2 3 4 5

SOCIAL MEDIA USE
1 2 3 4 5

CONNECTING WITH OTHERS
1 2 3 4 5

WORK TOWARDS A BIG GOAL
1 2 3 4 5

SENSE OF SATISFACTION
1 2 3 4 5

How could I have done better?

Overflow from today

Intention for tomorrow

What happened today?

DAY M T W T F S S

DATE / /

My Awareness

Mindful observations

1.

2.

3.

I am grateful for

Today, I felt most connected to the

PAST PRESENT FUTURE

Body Connect

How did I feel in my body?

TIRED
WEAK
SLOW
CAPABLE
STRONG
MOBILE
ENERGISED

How did I do today?

WATER
1 2 3 4 5

FOOD
1 2 3 4 5

ALCOHOL
1 2 3 4 5

EXERCISE
1 2 3 4 5

STRETCHING
1 2 3 4 5

MEDITATION
1 2 3 4 5

Physical highlight

Two-word check in

TODAY WAS A

/10

My Feelings

My morning mood was

- TIRED
- SLEEPY
- STRESSED
- PESSIMISTIC
- AVERAGE
- EXCITED
- OPTIMISTIC
- CALM

Dominant feeling today

Challenging feeling (and why)

Best feeling (and why)

My Way

How did I do today?

SET INTENTION
1 2 3 4 5

MORNING RITUAL
1 2 3 4 5

SOCIAL MEDIA USE
1 2 3 4 5

CONNECTING WITH OTHERS
1 2 3 4 5

WORK TOWARDS A BIG GOAL
1 2 3 4 5

SENSE OF SATISFACTION
1 2 3 4 5

How could I have done better?

Overflow from today

Intention for tomorrow

What happened today?

DAY M T W T F S S

DATE / /

My Awareness

Mindful observations

1.

2.

3.

I am grateful for

Today, I felt most connected to the

PAST PRESENT FUTURE

Body Connect

How did I feel in my body?

TIRED WEAK SLOW CAPABLE STRONG MOBILE ENERGISED

How did I do today?

WATER
1 2 3 4 5

FOOD
1 2 3 4 5

ALCOHOL
1 2 3 4 5

EXERCISE
1 2 3 4 5

STRETCHING
1 2 3 4 5

MEDITATION
1 2 3 4 5

Physical highlight

Two-word check in

TODAY WAS A
/10

My Feelings

My morning mood was

- TIRED
- SLEEPY
- STRESSED
- PESSIMISTIC
- AVERAGE
- EXCITED
- OPTIMISTIC
- CALM

Dominant feeling today

Challenging feeling (and why)

Best feeling (and why)

My Way

How did I do today?

SET INTENTION
1 2 3 4 5

MORNING RITUAL
1 2 3 4 5

SOCIAL MEDIA USE
1 2 3 4 5

CONNECTING WITH OTHERS
1 2 3 4 5

WORK TOWARDS A BIG GOAL
1 2 3 4 5

SENSE OF SATISFACTION
1 2 3 4 5

How could I have done better?

Overflow from today

Intention for tomorrow

What happened today?

DAY M T W T F S S

DATE / /

My Awareness

Mindful observations

1.

2.

3.

I am grateful for

Today, I felt most connected to the

◯ PAST ◯ PRESENT ◯ FUTURE

Body Connect

How did I feel in my body?

TIRED WEAK SLOW CAPABLE STRONG MOBILE ENERGISED

How did I do today?

WATER

1 2 3 4 5

FOOD

1 2 3 4 5

ALCOHOL

1 2 3 4 5

EXERCISE

1 2 3 4 5

STRETCHING

1 2 3 4 5

MEDITATION

1 2 3 4 5

Physical highlight

Two-word check in

TODAY WAS A /10

My Feelings

My morning mood was

- TIRED
- SLEEPY
- STRESSED
- PESSIMISTIC
- AVERAGE
- EXCITED
- OPTIMISTIC
- CALM

Dominant feeling today

Challenging feeling (and why)

Best feeling (and why)

My Way

How did I do today?

SET INTENTION
1 2 3 4 5

MORNING RITUAL
1 2 3 4 5

SOCIAL MEDIA USE
1 2 3 4 5

CONNECTING WITH OTHERS
1 2 3 4 5

WORK TOWARDS A BIG GOAL
1 2 3 4 5

SENSE OF SATISFACTION
1 2 3 4 5

How could I have done better?

Overflow from today

Intention for tomorrow

What happened today?

DAY M T W T F S S

DATE / /

My Awareness

Mindful observations

1.

2.

3.

I am grateful for

Today, I felt most connected to the

PAST PRESENT FUTURE

Body Connect

How did I feel in my body?

TIRED WEAK SLOW CAPABLE STRONG MOBILE ENERGISED

How did I do today?

WATER
1 2 3 4 5

FOOD
1 2 3 4 5

ALCOHOL
1 2 3 4 5

EXERCISE
1 2 3 4 5

STRETCHING
1 2 3 4 5

MEDITATION
1 2 3 4 5

Physical highlight

Two-word check in

TODAY WAS A
/10

My Feelings

My morning mood was

- TIRED
- SLEEPY
- STRESSED
- PESSIMISTIC
- AVERAGE
- EXCITED
- OPTIMISTIC
- CALM

Dominant feeling today

Challenging feeling (and why)

Best feeling (and why)

My Way

How did I do today?

SET INTENTION
1 2 3 4 5

MORNING RITUAL
1 2 3 4 5

SOCIAL MEDIA USE
1 2 3 4 5

CONNECTING WITH OTHERS
1 2 3 4 5

WORK TOWARDS A BIG GOAL
1 2 3 4 5

SENSE OF SATISFACTION
1 2 3 4 5

How could I have done better?

Overflow from today

Intention for tomorrow

What happened today?

DAY M T W T F S S

DATE / /

My Awareness

Mindful observations

1.

2.

3.

I am grateful for

Today, I felt most connected to the

◯ PAST ◯ PRESENT ◯ FUTURE

Body Connect

How did I feel in my body?

TIRED WEAK SLOW CAPABLE STRONG MOBILE ENERGISED

How did I do today?

WATER
1 2 3 4 5

FOOD
1 2 3 4 5

ALCOHOL
1 2 3 4 5

EXERCISE
1 2 3 4 5

STRETCHING
1 2 3 4 5

MEDITATION
1 2 3 4 5

Physical highlight

Two-word check in

TODAY WAS A

/10

My Feelings

My morning mood was

- TIRED
- SLEEPY
- STRESSED
- PESSIMISTIC
- AVERAGE
- EXCITED
- OPTIMISTIC
- CALM

Dominant feeling today

Challenging feeling (and why)

Best feeling (and why)

My Way

How did I do today?

SET INTENTION
1 2 3 4 5

MORNING RITUAL
1 2 3 4 5

SOCIAL MEDIA USE
1 2 3 4 5

CONNECTING WITH OTHERS
1 2 3 4 5

WORK TOWARDS A BIG GOAL
1 2 3 4 5

SENSE OF SATISFACTION
1 2 3 4 5

How could I have done better?

Overflow from today

Intention for tomorrow

What happened today?

DAY M T W T F S S

DATE / /

My Awareness

Mindful observations

1.

2.

3.

I am grateful for

Today, I felt most connected to the

PAST PRESENT FUTURE

Body Connect

How did I feel in my body?

TIRED

WEAK

SLOW

CAPABLE

STRONG

MOBILE

ENERGISED

How did I do today?

WATER
1 2 3 4 5

FOOD
1 2 3 4 5

ALCOHOL
1 2 3 4 5

EXERCISE
1 2 3 4 5

STRETCHING
1 2 3 4 5

MEDITATION
1 2 3 4 5

Physical highlight

Two-word check in

TODAY WAS A
/10

My Feelings

My morning mood was

- TIRED
- SLEEPY
- STRESSED
- PESSIMISTIC
- AVERAGE
- EXCITED
- OPTIMISTIC
- CALM

Dominant feeling today

Challenging feeling (and why)

Best feeling (and why)

My Way

How did I do today?

SET INTENTION
1 2 3 4 5

MORNING RITUAL
1 2 3 4 5

SOCIAL MEDIA USE
1 2 3 4 5

CONNECTING WITH OTHERS
1 2 3 4 5

WORK TOWARDS A BIG GOAL
1 2 3 4 5

SENSE OF SATISFACTION
1 2 3 4 5

How could I have done better?

Overflow from today

Intention for tomorrow

What happened today?

DAY M T W T F S S

DATE / /

My Awareness

Mindful observations

1.

2.

3.

I am grateful for

Today, I felt most connected to the

PAST PRESENT FUTURE

Body Connect

How did I feel in my body?

TIRED WEAK SLOW CAPABLE STRONG MOBILE ENERGISED

How did I do today?

WATER
1 2 3 4 5

FOOD
1 2 3 4 5

ALCOHOL
1 2 3 4 5

EXERCISE
1 2 3 4 5

STRETCHING
1 2 3 4 5

MEDITATION
1 2 3 4 5

Physical highlight

Two-word check in

TODAY WAS A

/10

My Feelings

My morning mood was

- TIRED
- SLEEPY
- STRESSED
- PESSIMISTIC
- AVERAGE
- EXCITED
- OPTIMISTIC
- CALM

Dominant feeling today

Challenging feeling (and why)

Best feeling (and why)

My Way

How did I do today?

SET INTENTION
1 2 3 4 5

MORNING RITUAL
1 2 3 4 5

SOCIAL MEDIA USE
1 2 3 4 5

CONNECTING WITH OTHERS
1 2 3 4 5

WORK TOWARDS A BIG GOAL
1 2 3 4 5

SENSE OF SATISFACTION
1 2 3 4 5

How could I have done better?

Overflow from today

Intention for tomorrow

What happened today?

DAY M T W T F S S

DATE / /

My Awareness

Mindful observations

1.

2.

3.

I am grateful for

Today, I felt most connected to the

PAST PRESENT FUTURE

Body Connect

How did I feel in my body?

- TIRED
- WEAK
- SLOW
- CAPABLE
- STRONG
- MOBILE
- ENERGISED

How did I do today?

WATER
1 2 3 4 5

FOOD
1 2 3 4 5

ALCOHOL
1 2 3 4 5

EXERCISE
1 2 3 4 5

STRETCHING
1 2 3 4 5

MEDITATION
1 2 3 4 5

Physical highlight

Two-word check in

TODAY WAS A
/10

My Feelings

My morning mood was

- TIRED
- SLEEPY
- STRESSED
- PESSIMISTIC
- AVERAGE
- EXCITED
- OPTIMISTIC
- CALM

Dominant feeling today

Challenging feeling (and why)

Best feeling (and why)

My Way

How did I do today?

SET INTENTION
1 2 3 4 5

MORNING RITUAL
1 2 3 4 5

SOCIAL MEDIA USE
1 2 3 4 5

CONNECTING WITH OTHERS
1 2 3 4 5

WORK TOWARDS A BIG GOAL
1 2 3 4 5

SENSE OF SATISFACTION
1 2 3 4 5

How could I have done better?

Overflow from today

Intention for tomorrow

What happened today?

DAY M T W T F S S

DATE / /

My Awareness

Mindful observations

1.

2.

3.

I am grateful for

Today, I felt most connected to the

PAST PRESENT FUTURE

Body Connect

How did I feel in my body?

TIRED WEAK SLOW CAPABLE STRONG MOBILE ENERGISED

How did I do today?

WATER
1 2 3 4 5

FOOD
1 2 3 4 5

ALCOHOL
1 2 3 4 5

EXERCISE
1 2 3 4 5

STRETCHING
1 2 3 4 5

MEDITATION
1 2 3 4 5

Physical highlight

Two-word check in

TODAY WAS A

/10

My Feelings

My morning mood was

- TIRED
- SLEEPY
- STRESSED
- PESSIMISTIC
- AVERAGE
- EXCITED
- OPTIMISTIC
- CALM

Dominant feeling today

Challenging feeling (and why)

Best feeling (and why)

My Way

How did I do today?

SET INTENTION
1 2 3 4 5

MORNING RITUAL
1 2 3 4 5

SOCIAL MEDIA USE
1 2 3 4 5

CONNECTING WITH OTHERS
1 2 3 4 5

WORK TOWARDS A BIG GOAL
1 2 3 4 5

SENSE OF SATISFACTION
1 2 3 4 5

How could I have done better?

Overflow from today

Intention for tomorrow

What happened today?

DAY M T W T F S S

DATE / /

My Awareness

Mindful observations

1.

2.

3.

I am grateful for

Today, I felt most connected to the

◯ PAST ◯ PRESENT ◯ FUTURE

Body Connect

How did I feel in my body?

TIRED WEAK SLOW CAPABLE STRONG MOBILE ENERGISED

How did I do today?

WATER
1 2 3 4 5

FOOD
1 2 3 4 5

ALCOHOL
1 2 3 4 5

EXERCISE
1 2 3 4 5

STRETCHING
1 2 3 4 5

MEDITATION
1 2 3 4 5

Physical highlight

Two-word check in

TODAY WAS A /10

My Feelings

My morning mood was

- TIRED
- SLEEPY
- STRESSED
- PESSIMISTIC
- AVERAGE
- EXCITED
- OPTIMISTIC
- CALM

Dominant feeling today

Challenging feeling (and why)

Best feeling (and why)

My Way

How did I do today?

SET INTENTION
1 2 3 4 5

MORNING RITUAL
1 2 3 4 5

SOCIAL MEDIA USE
1 2 3 4 5

CONNECTING WITH OTHERS
1 2 3 4 5

WORK TOWARDS A BIG GOAL
1 2 3 4 5

SENSE OF SATISFACTION
1 2 3 4 5

How could I have done better?

Overflow from today

Intention for tomorrow

What happened today?

DAY M T W T F S S

DATE / /

My Awareness

Mindful observations

1.

2.

3.

I am grateful for

Today, I felt most connected to the

PAST PRESENT FUTURE

Body Connect

How did I feel in my body?

TIRED
WEAK
SLOW
CAPABLE
STRONG
MOBILE
ENERGISED

How did I do today?

WATER
1 2 3 4 5

FOOD
1 2 3 4 5

ALCOHOL
1 2 3 4 5

EXERCISE
1 2 3 4 5

STRETCHING
1 2 3 4 5

MEDITATION
1 2 3 4 5

Physical highlight

Two-word check in

TODAY WAS A

/10

My Feelings

My morning mood was

- TIRED
- SLEEPY
- STRESSED
- PESSIMISTIC
- AVERAGE
- EXCITED
- OPTIMISTIC
- CALM

Dominant feeling today

Challenging feeling (and why)

Best feeling (and why)

My Way

How did I do today?

SET INTENTION
1 2 3 4 5

MORNING RITUAL
1 2 3 4 5

SOCIAL MEDIA USE
1 2 3 4 5

CONNECTING WITH OTHERS
1 2 3 4 5

WORK TOWARDS A BIG GOAL
1 2 3 4 5

SENSE OF SATISFACTION
1 2 3 4 5

How could I have done better?

Overflow from today

Intention for tomorrow

What happened today?

DAY M T W T F S S

DATE / /

My Awareness

Mindful observations

1.

2.

3.

I am grateful for

Today, I felt most connected to the

PAST PRESENT FUTURE

Body Connect

How did I feel in my body?

TIRED WEAK SLOW CAPABLE STRONG MOBILE ENERGISED

How did I do today?

WATER
1 2 3 4 5

FOOD
1 2 3 4 5

ALCOHOL
1 2 3 4 5

EXERCISE
1 2 3 4 5

STRETCHING
1 2 3 4 5

MEDITATION
1 2 3 4 5

Physical highlight

Two-word check in

TODAY WAS A
/10

My Feelings

My morning mood was

- TIRED
- SLEEPY
- STRESSED
- PESSIMISTIC
- AVERAGE
- EXCITED
- OPTIMISTIC
- CALM

Dominant feeling today

Challenging feeling (and why)

Best feeling (and why)

My Way

How did I do today?

SET INTENTION
1 2 3 4 5

MORNING RITUAL
1 2 3 4 5

SOCIAL MEDIA USE
1 2 3 4 5

CONNECTING WITH OTHERS
1 2 3 4 5

WORK TOWARDS A BIG GOAL
1 2 3 4 5

SENSE OF SATISFACTION
1 2 3 4 5

How could I have done better?

Overflow from today

Intention for tomorrow

What happened today?

DAY M T W T F S S

DATE / /

My Awareness

Mindful observations

1.

2.

3.

I am grateful for

Today, I felt most connected to the

PAST PRESENT FUTURE

Body Connect

How did I feel in my body?

TIRED WEAK SLOW CAPABLE STRONG MOBILE ENERGISED

How did I do today?

WATER
1 2 3 4 5

FOOD
1 2 3 4 5

ALCOHOL
1 2 3 4 5

EXERCISE
1 2 3 4 5

STRETCHING
1 2 3 4 5

MEDITATION
1 2 3 4 5

Physical highlight

Two-word check in

TODAY WAS A

/10

My Feelings

My morning mood was

- TIRED
- SLEEPY
- STRESSED
- PESSIMISTIC
- AVERAGE
- EXCITED
- OPTIMISTIC
- CALM

Dominant feeling today

Challenging feeling (and why)

Best feeling (and why)

My Way

How did I do today?

SET INTENTION
1 2 3 4 5

MORNING RITUAL
1 2 3 4 5

SOCIAL MEDIA USE
1 2 3 4 5

CONNECTING WITH OTHERS
1 2 3 4 5

WORK TOWARDS A BIG GOAL
1 2 3 4 5

SENSE OF SATISFACTION
1 2 3 4 5

How could I have done better?

Overflow from today

Intention for tomorrow

What happened today?

DAY M T W T F S S

DATE / /

My Awareness

Mindful observations

1.

2.

3.

I am grateful for

Today, I felt most connected to the

PAST PRESENT FUTURE

Body Connect

How did I feel in my body?

TIRED
WEAK
SLOW
CAPABLE
STRONG
MOBILE
ENERGISED

How did I do today?

WATER
1 2 3 4 5

FOOD
1 2 3 4 5

ALCOHOL
1 2 3 4 5

EXERCISE
1 2 3 4 5

STRETCHING
1 2 3 4 5

MEDITATION
1 2 3 4 5

Physical highlight

Two-word check in

TODAY WAS A

/10

My Feelings

My morning mood was

- TIRED
- SLEEPY
- STRESSED
- PESSIMISTIC
- AVERAGE
- EXCITED
- OPTIMISTIC
- CALM

Dominant feeling today

Challenging feeling (and why)

Best feeling (and why)

My Way

How did I do today?

SET INTENTION
1 2 3 4 5

MORNING RITUAL
1 2 3 4 5

SOCIAL MEDIA USE
1 2 3 4 5

CONNECTING WITH OTHERS
1 2 3 4 5

WORK TOWARDS A BIG GOAL
1 2 3 4 5

SENSE OF SATISFACTION
1 2 3 4 5

How could I have done better?

Overflow from today

Intention for tomorrow

What happened today?

DAY M T W T F S S

DATE / /

My Awareness

Mindful observations

1.

2.

3.

I am grateful for

Today, I felt most connected to the

PAST PRESENT FUTURE

Body Connect

How did I feel in my body?

TIRED
WEAK
SLOW
CAPABLE
STRONG
MOBILE
ENERGISED

How did I do today?

WATER
1 2 3 4 5

FOOD
1 2 3 4 5

ALCOHOL
1 2 3 4 5

EXERCISE
1 2 3 4 5

STRETCHING
1 2 3 4 5

MEDITATION
1 2 3 4 5

Physical highlight

Two-word check in

TODAY WAS A
/10

My Feelings

My morning mood was

- TIRED
- SLEEPY
- STRESSED
- PESSIMISTIC
- AVERAGE
- EXCITED
- OPTIMISTIC
- CALM

Dominant feeling today

Challenging feeling (and why)

Best feeling (and why)

My Way

How did I do today?

SET INTENTION
1 2 3 4 5

MORNING RITUAL
1 2 3 4 5

SOCIAL MEDIA USE
1 2 3 4 5

CONNECTING WITH OTHERS
1 2 3 4 5

WORK TOWARDS A BIG GOAL
1 2 3 4 5

SENSE OF SATISFACTION
1 2 3 4 5

How could I have done better?

Overflow from today

Intention for tomorrow

What happened today?

DAY M T W T F S S

DATE / /

My Awareness

Mindful observations

1.

2.

3.

I am grateful for

Today, I felt most connected to the

PAST PRESENT FUTURE

Body Connect

How did I feel in my body?

TIRED
WEAK
SLOW
CAPABLE
STRONG
MOBILE
ENERGISED

How did I do today?

WATER
1 2 3 4 5

FOOD
1 2 3 4 5

ALCOHOL
1 2 3 4 5

EXERCISE
1 2 3 4 5

STRETCHING
1 2 3 4 5

MEDITATION
1 2 3 4 5

Physical highlight

Two-word check in

TODAY WAS A
/10

My Feelings

My morning mood was

- TIRED
- SLEEPY
- STRESSED
- PESSIMISTIC
- AVERAGE
- EXCITED
- OPTIMISTIC
- CALM

Dominant feeling today

Challenging feeling (and why)

Best feeling (and why)

My Way

How did I do today?

SET INTENTION
1 2 3 4 5

MORNING RITUAL
1 2 3 4 5

SOCIAL MEDIA USE
1 2 3 4 5

CONNECTING WITH OTHERS
1 2 3 4 5

WORK TOWARDS A BIG GOAL
1 2 3 4 5

SENSE OF SATISFACTION
1 2 3 4 5

How could I have done better?

Overflow from today

Intention for tomorrow

What happened today?

DAY M T W T F S S

DATE / /

My Awareness

Mindful observations

1.

2.

3.

I am grateful for

Today, I felt most connected to the

◯ PAST ◯ ♥ PRESENT ◯ FUTURE

Body Connect

How did I feel in my body?

TIRED • WEAK • SLOW • CAPABLE • STRONG • MOBILE • ENERGISED

How did I do today?

WATER
1 2 3 4 5

FOOD
1 2 3 4 5

ALCOHOL
1 2 3 4 5

EXERCISE
1 2 3 4 5

STRETCHING
1 2 3 4 5

MEDITATION
1 2 3 4 5

Physical highlight

Two-word check in

TODAY WAS A

/10

My Feelings

My morning mood was

- TIRED
- SLEEPY
- STRESSED
- PESSIMISTIC
- AVERAGE
- EXCITED
- OPTIMISTIC
- CALM

Dominant feeling today

Challenging feeling (and why)

Best feeling (and why)

My Way

How did I do today?

SET INTENTION
1 2 3 4 5

MORNING RITUAL
1 2 3 4 5

SOCIAL MEDIA USE
1 2 3 4 5

CONNECTING WITH OTHERS
1 2 3 4 5

WORK TOWARDS A BIG GOAL
1 2 3 4 5

SENSE OF SATISFACTION
1 2 3 4 5

How could I have done better?

Overflow from today

Intention for tomorrow

What happened today?

DAY M T W T F S S

DATE / /

My Awareness

Mindful observations

1.

2.

3.

I am grateful for

Today, I felt most connected to the

◯ PAST ◯ PRESENT ◯ FUTURE

Body Connect

How did I feel in my body?

- TIRED
- WEAK
- SLOW
- CAPABLE
- STRONG
- MOBILE
- ENERGISED

How did I do today?

WATER
1 2 3 4 5

FOOD
1 2 3 4 5

ALCOHOL
1 2 3 4 5

EXERCISE
1 2 3 4 5

STRETCHING
1 2 3 4 5

MEDITATION
1 2 3 4 5

Physical highlight

Two-word check in

TODAY WAS A
/10

My Feelings

My morning mood was

- TIRED
- SLEEPY
- STRESSED
- PESSIMISTIC
- AVERAGE
- EXCITED
- OPTIMISTIC
- CALM

Dominant feeling today

Challenging feeling (and why)

Best feeling (and why)

My Way

How did I do today?

SET INTENTION
1 2 3 4 5

MORNING RITUAL
1 2 3 4 5

SOCIAL MEDIA USE
1 2 3 4 5

CONNECTING WITH OTHERS
1 2 3 4 5

WORK TOWARDS A BIG GOAL
1 2 3 4 5

SENSE OF SATISFACTION
1 2 3 4 5

How could I have done better?

Overflow from today

Intention for tomorrow

What happened today?

DAY M T W T F S S

DATE / /

My Awareness

Mindful observations

1.

2.

3.

I am grateful for

Today, I felt most connected to the

PAST PRESENT FUTURE

Body Connect

How did I feel in my body?

TIRED WEAK SLOW CAPABLE STRONG MOBILE ENERGISED

How did I do today?

WATER
1 2 3 4 5

FOOD
1 2 3 4 5

ALCOHOL
1 2 3 4 5

EXERCISE
1 2 3 4 5

STRETCHING
1 2 3 4 5

MEDITATION
1 2 3 4 5

Physical highlight

Two-word check in

TODAY WAS A
/10

My Feelings

My morning mood was

- TIRED
- SLEEPY
- STRESSED
- PESSIMISTIC
- AVERAGE
- EXCITED
- OPTIMISTIC
- CALM

Dominant feeling today

Challenging feeling (and why)

Best feeling (and why)

My Way

How did I do today?

SET INTENTION
1 2 3 4 5

MORNING RITUAL
1 2 3 4 5

SOCIAL MEDIA USE
1 2 3 4 5

CONNECTING WITH OTHERS
1 2 3 4 5

WORK TOWARDS A BIG GOAL
1 2 3 4 5

SENSE OF SATISFACTION
1 2 3 4 5

How could I have done better?

Overflow from today

Intention for tomorrow

What happened today?

DAY M T W T F S S

DATE / /

My Awareness

Mindful observations

1.

2.

3.

I am grateful for

Today, I felt most connected to the

PAST PRESENT FUTURE

Body Connect

How did I feel in my body?

- TIRED
- WEAK
- SLOW
- CAPABLE
- STRONG
- MOBILE
- ENERGISED

How did I do today?

WATER
1 2 3 4 5

FOOD
1 2 3 4 5

ALCOHOL
1 2 3 4 5

EXERCISE
1 2 3 4 5

STRETCHING
1 2 3 4 5

MEDITATION
1 2 3 4 5

Physical highlight

Two-word check in

TODAY WAS A
/10

My Feelings

My morning mood was

- TIRED
- SLEEPY
- STRESSED
- PESSIMISTIC
- AVERAGE
- EXCITED
- OPTIMISTIC
- CALM

Dominant feeling today

Challenging feeling (and why)

Best feeling (and why)

My Way

How did I do today?

SET INTENTION
1 2 3 4 5

MORNING RITUAL
1 2 3 4 5

SOCIAL MEDIA USE
1 2 3 4 5

CONNECTING WITH OTHERS
1 2 3 4 5

WORK TOWARDS A BIG GOAL
1 2 3 4 5

SENSE OF SATISFACTION
1 2 3 4 5

How could I have done better?

Overflow from today

Intention for tomorrow

What happened today?

DAY M T W T F S S

DATE / /

My Awareness

Mindful observations

1.

2.

3.

I am grateful for

Today, I felt most connected to the

◯ PAST ◯ PRESENT ◯ FUTURE

Body Connect

How did I feel in my body?

TIRED WEAK SLOW CAPABLE STRONG MOBILE ENERGISED

How did I do today?

WATER
1 2 3 4 5

FOOD
1 2 3 4 5

ALCOHOL
1 2 3 4 5

EXERCISE
1 2 3 4 5

STRETCHING
1 2 3 4 5

MEDITATION
1 2 3 4 5

Physical highlight

Two-word check in

TODAY WAS A
/10

My Feelings

My morning mood was

- TIRED
- SLEEPY
- STRESSED
- PESSIMISTIC
- AVERAGE
- EXCITED
- OPTIMISTIC
- CALM

Dominant feeling today

Challenging feeling (and why)

Best feeling (and why)

My Way

How did I do today?

SET INTENTION
1 2 3 4 5

MORNING RITUAL
1 2 3 4 5

SOCIAL MEDIA USE
1 2 3 4 5

CONNECTING WITH OTHERS
1 2 3 4 5

WORK TOWARDS A BIG GOAL
1 2 3 4 5

SENSE OF SATISFACTION
1 2 3 4 5

How could I have done better?

Overflow from today

Intention for tomorrow

What happened today?

DAY M T W T F S S

DATE / /

My Awareness

Mindful observations

1.

2.

3.

I am grateful for

Today, I felt most connected to the

PAST PRESENT FUTURE

Body Connect

How did I feel in my body?

- TIRED
- WEAK
- SLOW
- CAPABLE
- STRONG
- MOBILE
- ENERGISED

How did I do today?

WATER
1 2 3 4 5

FOOD
1 2 3 4 5

ALCOHOL
1 2 3 4 5

EXERCISE
1 2 3 4 5

STRETCHING
1 2 3 4 5

MEDITATION
1 2 3 4 5

Physical highlight

Two-word check in

TODAY WAS A

/10

My Feelings

My morning mood was

- TIRED
- SLEEPY
- STRESSED
- PESSIMISTIC
- AVERAGE
- EXCITED
- OPTIMISTIC
- CALM

Dominant feeling today

Challenging feeling (and why)

Best feeling (and why)

My Way

How did I do today?

SET INTENTION
1 2 3 4 5

MORNING RITUAL
1 2 3 4 5

SOCIAL MEDIA USE
1 2 3 4 5

CONNECTING WITH OTHERS
1 2 3 4 5

WORK TOWARDS A BIG GOAL
1 2 3 4 5

SENSE OF SATISFACTION
1 2 3 4 5

How could I have done better?

Overflow from today

Intention for tomorrow

What happened today?

DAY M T W T F S S

DATE / /

My Awareness

Mindful observations

1.

2.

3.

I am grateful for

Today, I felt most connected to the

○ PAST ○ PRESENT ○ FUTURE

Body Connect

How did I feel in my body?

TIRED · WEAK · SLOW · CAPABLE · STRONG · MOBILE · ENERGISED

How did I do today?

WATER
1 2 3 4 5

FOOD
1 2 3 4 5

ALCOHOL
1 2 3 4 5

EXERCISE
1 2 3 4 5

STRETCHING
1 2 3 4 5

MEDITATION
1 2 3 4 5

Physical highlight

Two-word check in

TODAY WAS A

/10

My Feelings

My morning mood was

- TIRED
- SLEEPY
- STRESSED
- PESSIMISTIC
- AVERAGE
- EXCITED
- OPTIMISTIC
- CALM

Dominant feeling today

Challenging feeling (and why)

Best feeling (and why)

My Way

How did I do today?

SET INTENTION
1 2 3 4 5

MORNING RITUAL
1 2 3 4 5

SOCIAL MEDIA USE
1 2 3 4 5

CONNECTING WITH OTHERS
1 2 3 4 5

WORK TOWARDS A BIG GOAL
1 2 3 4 5

SENSE OF SATISFACTION
1 2 3 4 5

How could I have done better?

Overflow from today

Intention for tomorrow

What happened today?

DAY M T W T F S S

DATE / /

My Awareness

Mindful observations

1.

2.

3.

I am grateful for

Today, I felt most connected to the

PAST PRESENT FUTURE

Body Connect

How did I feel in my body?

TIRED
WEAK
SLOW
CAPABLE
STRONG
MOBILE
ENERGISED

How did I do today?

WATER	1	2	3	4	5
FOOD	1	2	3	4	5
ALCOHOL	1	2	3	4	5
EXERCISE	1	2	3	4	5
STRETCHING	1	2	3	4	5
MEDITATION	1	2	3	4	5

Physical highlight

Two-word check in

TODAY WAS A

/10

My Feelings

My morning mood was

- TIRED
- SLEEPY
- STRESSED
- PESSIMISTIC
- AVERAGE
- EXCITED
- OPTIMISTIC
- CALM

Dominant feeling today

Challenging feeling (and why)

Best feeling (and why)

My Way

How did I do today?

SET INTENTION
1 2 3 4 5

MORNING RITUAL
1 2 3 4 5

SOCIAL MEDIA USE
1 2 3 4 5

CONNECTING WITH OTHERS
1 2 3 4 5

WORK TOWARDS A BIG GOAL
1 2 3 4 5

SENSE OF SATISFACTION
1 2 3 4 5

How could I have done better?

Overflow from today

Intention for tomorrow

What happened today?

DAY M T W T F S S

DATE / /

My Awareness

Mindful observations

1.

2.

3.

I am grateful for

Today, I felt most connected to the

PAST PRESENT FUTURE

Body Connect

How did I feel in my body?

TIRED WEAK SLOW CAPABLE STRONG MOBILE ENERGISED

How did I do today?

WATER
1 2 3 4 5

FOOD
1 2 3 4 5

ALCOHOL
1 2 3 4 5

EXERCISE
1 2 3 4 5

STRETCHING
1 2 3 4 5

MEDITATION
1 2 3 4 5

Physical highlight

Two-word check in

TODAY WAS A /10

My Feelings

My morning mood was

- TIRED
- SLEEPY
- STRESSED
- PESSIMISTIC
- AVERAGE
- EXCITED
- OPTIMISTIC
- CALM

Dominant feeling today

Challenging feeling (and why)

Best feeling (and why)

My Way

How did I do today?

SET INTENTION
1 2 3 4 5

MORNING RITUAL
1 2 3 4 5

SOCIAL MEDIA USE
1 2 3 4 5

CONNECTING WITH OTHERS
1 2 3 4 5

WORK TOWARDS A BIG GOAL
1 2 3 4 5

SENSE OF SATISFACTION
1 2 3 4 5

How could I have done better?

Overflow from today

Intention for tomorrow

What happened today?

DAY M T W T F S S

DATE / /

My Awareness

Mindful observations

1.

2.

3.

I am grateful for

Today, I felt most connected to the

PAST PRESENT FUTURE

Body Connect

How did I feel in my body?

TIRED WEAK SLOW CAPABLE STRONG MOBILE ENERGISED

How did I do today?

WATER
1 2 3 4 5

FOOD
1 2 3 4 5

ALCOHOL
1 2 3 4 5

EXERCISE
1 2 3 4 5

STRETCHING
1 2 3 4 5

MEDITATION
1 2 3 4 5

Physical highlight

Two-word check in

TODAY WAS A
/10

My Feelings

My morning mood was

- TIRED
- SLEEPY
- STRESSED
- PESSIMISTIC
- AVERAGE
- EXCITED
- OPTIMISTIC
- CALM

Dominant feeling today

Challenging feeling (and why)

Best feeling (and why)

My Way

How did I do today?

SET INTENTION
1 2 3 4 5

MORNING RITUAL
1 2 3 4 5

SOCIAL MEDIA USE
1 2 3 4 5

CONNECTING WITH OTHERS
1 2 3 4 5

WORK TOWARDS A BIG GOAL
1 2 3 4 5

SENSE OF SATISFACTION
1 2 3 4 5

How could I have done better?

Overflow from today

Intention for tomorrow

What happened today?

DAY M T W T F S S

DATE / /

My Awareness

Mindful observations

1.

2.

3.

I am grateful for

Today, I felt most connected to the

◯ PAST ◯ PRESENT ◯ FUTURE

Body Connect

How did I feel in my body?

- TIRED
- WEAK
- SLOW
- CAPABLE
- STRONG
- MOBILE
- ENERGISED

How did I do today?

WATER
1 2 3 4 5

FOOD
1 2 3 4 5

ALCOHOL
1 2 3 4 5

EXERCISE
1 2 3 4 5

STRETCHING
1 2 3 4 5

MEDITATION
1 2 3 4 5

Physical highlight

Two-word check in

TODAY WAS A
/10

My Feelings

My morning mood was

- TIRED
- SLEEPY
- STRESSED
- PESSIMISTIC
- AVERAGE
- EXCITED
- OPTIMISTIC
- CALM

Dominant feeling today

Challenging feeling (and why)

Best feeling (and why)

My Way

How did I do today?

SET INTENTION
1 2 3 4 5

MORNING RITUAL
1 2 3 4 5

SOCIAL MEDIA USE
1 2 3 4 5

CONNECTING WITH OTHERS
1 2 3 4 5

WORK TOWARDS A BIG GOAL
1 2 3 4 5

SENSE OF SATISFACTION
1 2 3 4 5

How could I have done better?

Overflow from today

Intention for tomorrow

What happened today?

DAY M T W T F S S

DATE / /

My Awareness

Mindful observations

1.

2.

3.

I am grateful for

Today, I felt most connected to the

PAST PRESENT FUTURE

Body Connect

How did I feel in my body?

TIRED WEAK SLOW CAPABLE STRONG MOBILE ENERGISED

How did I do today?

WATER
1 2 3 4 5

FOOD
1 2 3 4 5

ALCOHOL
1 2 3 4 5

EXERCISE
1 2 3 4 5

STRETCHING
1 2 3 4 5

MEDITATION
1 2 3 4 5

Physical highlight

Two-word check in

TODAY WAS A /10

My Feelings

My morning mood was

- TIRED
- SLEEPY
- STRESSED
- PESSIMISTIC
- AVERAGE
- EXCITED
- OPTIMISTIC
- CALM

Dominant feeling today

Challenging feeling (and why)

Best feeling (and why)

My Way

How did I do today?

SET INTENTION
1 2 3 4 5

MORNING RITUAL
1 2 3 4 5

SOCIAL MEDIA USE
1 2 3 4 5

CONNECTING WITH OTHERS
1 2 3 4 5

WORK TOWARDS A BIG GOAL
1 2 3 4 5

SENSE OF SATISFACTION
1 2 3 4 5

How could I have done better?

Overflow from today

Intention for tomorrow

What happened today?

DAY M T W T F S S

DATE / /

My Awareness

Mindful observations

1.

2.

3.

I am grateful for

Today, I felt most connected to the

◯ PAST ◯ ♥ PRESENT ◯ FUTURE

Body Connect

How did I feel in my body?

- TIRED
- WEAK
- SLOW
- CAPABLE
- STRONG
- MOBILE
- ENERGISED

How did I do today?

WATER
1 2 3 4 5

FOOD
1 2 3 4 5

ALCOHOL
1 2 3 4 5

EXERCISE
1 2 3 4 5

STRETCHING
1 2 3 4 5

MEDITATION
1 2 3 4 5

Physical highlight

Two-word check in

TODAY WAS A
/10

My Feelings

My morning mood was

- TIRED
- SLEEPY
- STRESSED
- PESSIMISTIC
- AVERAGE
- EXCITED
- OPTIMISTIC
- CALM

Dominant feeling today

Challenging feeling (and why)

Best feeling (and why)

My Way

How did I do today?

SET INTENTION
1 2 3 4 5

MORNING RITUAL
1 2 3 4 5

SOCIAL MEDIA USE
1 2 3 4 5

CONNECTING WITH OTHERS
1 2 3 4 5

WORK TOWARDS A BIG GOAL
1 2 3 4 5

SENSE OF SATISFACTION
1 2 3 4 5

How could I have done better?

Overflow from today

Intention for tomorrow

What happened today?

DAY M T W T F S S

DATE / /

My Awareness

Mindful observations

1.

2.

3.

I am grateful for

Today, I felt most connected to the

PAST PRESENT FUTURE

Body Connect

How did I feel in my body?

TIRED WEAK SLOW CAPABLE STRONG MOBILE ENERGISED

How did I do today?

WATER
1 2 3 4 5

FOOD
1 2 3 4 5

ALCOHOL
1 2 3 4 5

EXERCISE
1 2 3 4 5

STRETCHING
1 2 3 4 5

MEDITATION
1 2 3 4 5

Physical highlight

Two-word check in

TODAY WAS A
/10

My Feelings

My morning mood was

- TIRED
- SLEEPY
- STRESSED
- PESSIMISTIC
- AVERAGE
- EXCITED
- OPTIMISTIC
- CALM

Dominant feeling today

Challenging feeling (and why)

Best feeling (and why)

My Way

How did I do today?

SET INTENTION
1 2 3 4 5

MORNING RITUAL
1 2 3 4 5

SOCIAL MEDIA USE
1 2 3 4 5

CONNECTING WITH OTHERS
1 2 3 4 5

WORK TOWARDS A BIG GOAL
1 2 3 4 5

SENSE OF SATISFACTION
1 2 3 4 5

How could I have done better?

Overflow from today

Intention for tomorrow

What happened today?

DAY M T W T F S S

DATE / /

My Awareness

Mindful observations

1.

2.

3.

I am grateful for

Today, I felt most connected to the

PAST PRESENT FUTURE

Body Connect

How did I feel in my body?

TIRED
WEAK
SLOW
CAPABLE
STRONG
MOBILE
ENERGISED

How did I do today?

WATER
1 2 3 4 5

FOOD
1 2 3 4 5

ALCOHOL
1 2 3 4 5

EXERCISE
1 2 3 4 5

STRETCHING
1 2 3 4 5

MEDITATION
1 2 3 4 5

Physical highlight

Two-word check in

TODAY WAS A

/10

My Feelings

My morning mood was

- TIRED
- SLEEPY
- STRESSED
- PESSIMISTIC
- AVERAGE
- EXCITED
- OPTIMISTIC
- CALM

Dominant feeling today

Challenging feeling (and why)

Best feeling (and why)

My Way

How did I do today?

SET INTENTION
1 2 3 4 5

MORNING RITUAL
1 2 3 4 5

SOCIAL MEDIA USE
1 2 3 4 5

CONNECTING WITH OTHERS
1 2 3 4 5

WORK TOWARDS A BIG GOAL
1 2 3 4 5

SENSE OF SATISFACTION
1 2 3 4 5

How could I have done better?

Overflow from today

Intention for tomorrow

What happened today?

DAY M T W T F S S

DATE / /

My Awareness

Mindful observations

1.

2.

3.

I am grateful for

Today, I felt most connected to the

PAST PRESENT FUTURE

Body Connect

How did I feel in my body?

- TIRED
- WEAK
- SLOW
- CAPABLE
- STRONG
- MOBILE
- ENERGISED

How did I do today?

WATER
1 2 3 4 5

FOOD
1 2 3 4 5

ALCOHOL
1 2 3 4 5

EXERCISE
1 2 3 4 5

STRETCHING
1 2 3 4 5

MEDITATION
1 2 3 4 5

Physical highlight

Two-word check in

TODAY WAS A

/10

My Feelings

My morning mood was

- TIRED
- SLEEPY
- STRESSED
- PESSIMISTIC
- AVERAGE
- EXCITED
- OPTIMISTIC
- CALM

Dominant feeling today

Challenging feeling (and why)

Best feeling (and why)

My Way

How did I do today?

SET INTENTION
1 2 3 4 5

MORNING RITUAL
1 2 3 4 5

SOCIAL MEDIA USE
1 2 3 4 5

CONNECTING WITH OTHERS
1 2 3 4 5

WORK TOWARDS A BIG GOAL
1 2 3 4 5

SENSE OF SATISFACTION
1 2 3 4 5

How could I have done better?

Overflow from today

Intention for tomorrow

What happened today?

DAY M T W T F S S

DATE / /

My Awareness

Mindful observations

1.

2.

3.

I am grateful for

Today, I felt most connected to the

PAST PRESENT FUTURE

Body Connect

How did I feel in my body?

TIRED WEAK SLOW CAPABLE STRONG MOBILE ENERGISED

How did I do today?

WATER
1 2 3 4 5

FOOD
1 2 3 4 5

ALCOHOL
1 2 3 4 5

EXERCISE
1 2 3 4 5

STRETCHING
1 2 3 4 5

MEDITATION
1 2 3 4 5

Physical highlight

Two-word check in

TODAY WAS A

/10

My Feelings

My morning mood was

- TIRED
- SLEEPY
- STRESSED
- PESSIMISTIC
- AVERAGE
- EXCITED
- OPTIMISTIC
- CALM

Dominant feeling today

Challenging feeling (and why)

Best feeling (and why)

My Way

How did I do today?

SET INTENTION
1 2 3 4 5

MORNING RITUAL
1 2 3 4 5

SOCIAL MEDIA USE
1 2 3 4 5

CONNECTING WITH OTHERS
1 2 3 4 5

WORK TOWARDS A BIG GOAL
1 2 3 4 5

SENSE OF SATISFACTION
1 2 3 4 5

How could I have done better?

Overflow from today

Intention for tomorrow

What happened today?

DAY M T W T F S S

DATE / /

My Awareness

Mindful observations

1.

2.

3.

I am grateful for

Today, I felt most connected to the

○ PAST ○ PRESENT ○ FUTURE

Body Connect

How did I feel in my body?

- TIRED
- WEAK
- SLOW
- CAPABLE
- STRONG
- MOBILE
- ENERGISED

How did I do today?

WATER
1 2 3 4 5

FOOD
1 2 3 4 5

ALCOHOL
1 2 3 4 5

EXERCISE
1 2 3 4 5

STRETCHING
1 2 3 4 5

MEDITATION
1 2 3 4 5

Physical highlight

Two-word check in

TODAY WAS A
/10

My Feelings

My morning mood was

- TIRED
- SLEEPY
- STRESSED
- PESSIMISTIC
- AVERAGE
- EXCITED
- OPTIMISTIC
- CALM

Dominant feeling today

Challenging feeling (and why)

Best feeling (and why)

My Way

How did I do today?

SET INTENTION
1 2 3 4 5

MORNING RITUAL
1 2 3 4 5

SOCIAL MEDIA USE
1 2 3 4 5

CONNECTING WITH OTHERS
1 2 3 4 5

WORK TOWARDS A BIG GOAL
1 2 3 4 5

SENSE OF SATISFACTION
1 2 3 4 5

How could I have done better?

Overflow from today

Intention for tomorrow

What happened today?

DAY M T W T F S S

DATE / /

My Awareness

Mindful observations

1.

2.

3.

I am grateful for

Today, I felt most connected to the

PAST PRESENT FUTURE

Body Connect

How did I feel in my body?

TIRED
WEAK
SLOW
CAPABLE
STRONG
MOBILE
ENERGISED

How did I do today?

WATER
1 2 3 4 5

FOOD
1 2 3 4 5

ALCOHOL
1 2 3 4 5

EXERCISE
1 2 3 4 5

STRETCHING
1 2 3 4 5

MEDITATION
1 2 3 4 5

Physical highlight

Two-word check in

TODAY WAS A

/10

My Feelings

My morning mood was

- TIRED
- SLEEPY
- STRESSED
- PESSIMISTIC
- AVERAGE
- EXCITED
- OPTIMISTIC
- CALM

Dominant feeling today

Challenging feeling (and why)

Best feeling (and why)

My Way

How did I do today?

SET INTENTION
1 2 3 4 5

MORNING RITUAL
1 2 3 4 5

SOCIAL MEDIA USE
1 2 3 4 5

CONNECTING WITH OTHERS
1 2 3 4 5

WORK TOWARDS A BIG GOAL
1 2 3 4 5

SENSE OF SATISFACTION
1 2 3 4 5

How could I have done better?

Overflow from today

Intention for tomorrow

What happened today?

DAY M T W T F S S

DATE / /

My Awareness

Mindful observations

1.

2.

3.

I am grateful for

Today, I felt most connected to the

PAST PRESENT FUTURE

Body Connect

How did I feel in my body?

TIRED WEAK SLOW CAPABLE STRONG MOBILE ENERGISED

How did I do today?

WATER
1 2 3 4 5

FOOD
1 2 3 4 5

ALCOHOL
1 2 3 4 5

EXERCISE
1 2 3 4 5

STRETCHING
1 2 3 4 5

MEDITATION
1 2 3 4 5

Physical highlight

Two-word check in

TODAY WAS A

/10

My Feelings

My morning mood was

- TIRED
- SLEEPY
- STRESSED
- PESSIMISTIC
- AVERAGE
- EXCITED
- OPTIMISTIC
- CALM

Dominant feeling today

Challenging feeling (and why)

Best feeling (and why)

My Way

How did I do today?

SET INTENTION
1 2 3 4 5

MORNING RITUAL
1 2 3 4 5

SOCIAL MEDIA USE
1 2 3 4 5

CONNECTING WITH OTHERS
1 2 3 4 5

WORK TOWARDS A BIG GOAL
1 2 3 4 5

SENSE OF SATISFACTION
1 2 3 4 5

How could I have done better?

Overflow from today

Intention for tomorrow

What happened today?

DAY M T W T F S S

DATE / /

My Awareness

Mindful observations

1.

2.

3.

I am grateful for

Today, I felt most connected to the

◯ PAST ◯ PRESENT ◯ FUTURE

Body Connect

How did I feel in my body?

- TIRED
- WEAK
- SLOW
- CAPABLE
- STRONG
- MOBILE
- ENERGISED

How did I do today?

WATER
1 2 3 4 5

FOOD
1 2 3 4 5

ALCOHOL
1 2 3 4 5

EXERCISE
1 2 3 4 5

STRETCHING
1 2 3 4 5

MEDITATION
1 2 3 4 5

Physical highlight

Two-word check in

TODAY WAS A

/10

My Feelings

My morning mood was

- TIRED
- SLEEPY
- STRESSED
- PESSIMISTIC
- AVERAGE
- EXCITED
- OPTIMISTIC
- CALM

Dominant feeling today

Challenging feeling (and why)

Best feeling (and why)

My Way

How did I do today?

SET INTENTION

1 2 3 4 5

MORNING RITUAL

1 2 3 4 5

SOCIAL MEDIA USE

1 2 3 4 5

CONNECTING WITH OTHERS

1 2 3 4 5

WORK TOWARDS A BIG GOAL

1 2 3 4 5

SENSE OF SATISFACTION

1 2 3 4 5

How could I have done better?

Overflow from today

Intention for tomorrow

What happened today?

DAY M T W T F S S

DATE / /

My Awareness

Mindful observations

1.

2.

3.

I am grateful for

Today, I felt most connected to the

◯ PAST ◯ PRESENT ◯ FUTURE

Body Connect

How did I feel in my body?

TIRED · WEAK · SLOW · CAPABLE · STRONG · MOBILE · ENERGISED

How did I do today?

WATER
1 2 3 4 5

FOOD
1 2 3 4 5

ALCOHOL
1 2 3 4 5

EXERCISE
1 2 3 4 5

STRETCHING
1 2 3 4 5

MEDITATION
1 2 3 4 5

Physical highlight

Two-word check in

TODAY WAS A

/10

My Feelings

My morning mood was

- TIRED
- SLEEPY
- STRESSED
- PESSIMISTIC
- AVERAGE
- EXCITED
- OPTIMISTIC
- CALM

Dominant feeling today

Challenging feeling (and why)

Best feeling (and why)

My Way

How did I do today?

SET INTENTION
1 2 3 4 5

MORNING RITUAL
1 2 3 4 5

SOCIAL MEDIA USE
1 2 3 4 5

CONNECTING WITH OTHERS
1 2 3 4 5

WORK TOWARDS A BIG GOAL
1 2 3 4 5

SENSE OF SATISFACTION
1 2 3 4 5

How could I have done better?

Overflow from today

Intention for tomorrow

What happened today?

DAY M T W T F S S

DATE / /

My Awareness

Mindful observations

1.

2.

3.

I am grateful for

Today, I felt most connected to the

PAST PRESENT FUTURE

Body Connect

How did I feel in my body?

TIRED WEAK SLOW CAPABLE STRONG MOBILE ENERGISED

How did I do today?

WATER
1 2 3 4 5

FOOD
1 2 3 4 5

ALCOHOL
1 2 3 4 5

EXERCISE
1 2 3 4 5

STRETCHING
1 2 3 4 5

MEDITATION
1 2 3 4 5

Physical highlight

Two-word check in

TODAY WAS A

/10

My Feelings

My morning mood was

- TIRED
- SLEEPY
- STRESSED
- PESSIMISTIC
- AVERAGE
- EXCITED
- OPTIMISTIC
- CALM

Dominant feeling today

Challenging feeling (and why)

Best feeling (and why)

My Way

How did I do today?

SET INTENTION
1 2 3 4 5

MORNING RITUAL
1 2 3 4 5

SOCIAL MEDIA USE
1 2 3 4 5

CONNECTING WITH OTHERS
1 2 3 4 5

WORK TOWARDS A BIG GOAL
1 2 3 4 5

SENSE OF SATISFACTION
1 2 3 4 5

How could I have done better?

Overflow from today

Intention for tomorrow

What happened today?

DAY M T W T F S S

DATE / /

My Awareness

Mindful observations

1.

2.

3.

I am grateful for

Today, I felt most connected to the

PAST PRESENT FUTURE

Body Connect

How did I feel in my body?

TIRED WEAK SLOW CAPABLE STRONG MOBILE ENERGISED

How did I do today?

WATER
1 2 3 4 5

FOOD
1 2 3 4 5

ALCOHOL
1 2 3 4 5

EXERCISE
1 2 3 4 5

STRETCHING
1 2 3 4 5

MEDITATION
1 2 3 4 5

Physical highlight

Two-word check in

TODAY WAS A

/10

My Feelings

My morning mood was

- TIRED
- SLEEPY
- STRESSED
- PESSIMISTIC
- AVERAGE
- EXCITED
- OPTIMISTIC
- CALM

Dominant feeling today

Challenging feeling (and why)

Best feeling (and why)

My Way

How did I do today?

SET INTENTION
1 2 3 4 5

MORNING RITUAL
1 2 3 4 5

SOCIAL MEDIA USE
1 2 3 4 5

CONNECTING WITH OTHERS
1 2 3 4 5

WORK TOWARDS A BIG GOAL
1 2 3 4 5

SENSE OF SATISFACTION
1 2 3 4 5

How could I have done better?

Overflow from today

Intention for tomorrow

What happened today?

DAY M T W T F S S

DATE / /

My Awareness

Mindful observations

1.

2.

3.

I am grateful for

Today, I felt most connected to the

PAST PRESENT FUTURE

Body Connect

How did I feel in my body?

- TIRED
- WEAK
- SLOW
- CAPABLE
- STRONG
- MOBILE
- ENERGISED

How did I do today?

WATER
1 2 3 4 5

FOOD
1 2 3 4 5

ALCOHOL
1 2 3 4 5

EXERCISE
1 2 3 4 5

STRETCHING
1 2 3 4 5

MEDITATION
1 2 3 4 5

Physical highlight

Two-word check in

TODAY WAS A

/10

My Feelings

My morning mood was

- TIRED
- SLEEPY
- STRESSED
- PESSIMISTIC
- AVERAGE
- EXCITED
- OPTIMISTIC
- CALM

Dominant feeling today

Challenging feeling (and why)

Best feeling (and why)

My Way

How did I do today?

SET INTENTION
1 2 3 4 5

MORNING RITUAL
1 2 3 4 5

SOCIAL MEDIA USE
1 2 3 4 5

CONNECTING WITH OTHERS
1 2 3 4 5

WORK TOWARDS A BIG GOAL
1 2 3 4 5

SENSE OF SATISFACTION
1 2 3 4 5

How could I have done better?

Overflow from today

Intention for tomorrow

What happened today?

DAY M T W T F S S

DATE / /

My Awareness

Mindful observations

1.

2.

3.

I am grateful for

Today, I felt most connected to the

PAST PRESENT FUTURE

Body Connect

How did I feel in my body?

- TIRED
- WEAK
- SLOW
- CAPABLE
- STRONG
- MOBILE
- ENERGISED

How did I do today?

WATER
1 2 3 4 5

FOOD
1 2 3 4 5

ALCOHOL
1 2 3 4 5

EXERCISE
1 2 3 4 5

STRETCHING
1 2 3 4 5

MEDITATION
1 2 3 4 5

Physical highlight

Two-word check in

TODAY WAS A

/10

My Feelings

My morning mood was

- TIRED
- SLEEPY
- STRESSED
- PESSIMISTIC
- AVERAGE
- EXCITED
- OPTIMISTIC
- CALM

Dominant feeling today

Challenging feeling (and why)

Best feeling (and why)

My Way

How did I do today?

SET INTENTION
1 2 3 4 5

MORNING RITUAL
1 2 3 4 5

SOCIAL MEDIA USE
1 2 3 4 5

CONNECTING WITH OTHERS
1 2 3 4 5

WORK TOWARDS A BIG GOAL
1 2 3 4 5

SENSE OF SATISFACTION
1 2 3 4 5

How could I have done better?

Overflow from today

Intention for tomorrow

What happened today?

DAY M T W T F S S

DATE / /

My Awareness

Mindful observations

1.

2.

3.

I am grateful for

Today, I felt most connected to the

◯ PAST ◯ PRESENT ◯ FUTURE

Body Connect

How did I feel in my body?

- TIRED
- WEAK
- SLOW
- CAPABLE
- STRONG
- MOBILE
- ENERGISED

How did I do today?

WATER
1 2 3 4 5

FOOD
1 2 3 4 5

ALCOHOL
1 2 3 4 5

EXERCISE
1 2 3 4 5

STRETCHING
1 2 3 4 5

MEDITATION
1 2 3 4 5

Physical highlight

Two-word check in

TODAY WAS A

/10

My Feelings

My morning mood was

- TIRED
- SLEEPY
- STRESSED
- PESSIMISTIC
- AVERAGE
- EXCITED
- OPTIMISTIC
- CALM

Dominant feeling today

Challenging feeling (and why)

Best feeling (and why)

My Way

How did I do today?

SET INTENTION

1 2 3 4 5

MORNING RITUAL

1 2 3 4 5

SOCIAL MEDIA USE

1 2 3 4 5

CONNECTING WITH OTHERS

1 2 3 4 5

WORK TOWARDS A BIG GOAL

1 2 3 4 5

SENSE OF SATISFACTION

1 2 3 4 5

How could I have done better?

Overflow from today

Intention for tomorrow

Well Done.

Are you feeling better now?

HERRON

First Published in 2021 by Herron Book Distributors Pty Ltd,
This edition published 2022
14 Manton St
Morningside
QLD 4170
www.herronbooks.com

Captain Honey
WWW.CAPTAINHONEY.COM.AU

Custom book production by Captain Honey Pty Ltd
12 Station Street
Bangalow
NSW 2479
www.captainhoney.com.au

Cataloguing-in-Publication. A catalogue record for this book is available from the National Library of Australia

ISBN: 978-1-922432-91-9

Printed and bound in China

5 4 3 2 22 23 24 25